Sir Daniel Morris

The Colony of British Honduras

It's Resources and Prospects

Sir Daniel Morris

The Colony of British Honduras
It's Resources and Prospects

ISBN/EAN: 9783744692557

Printed in Europe, USA, Canada, Australia, Japan

Cover: Foto ©ninafisch / pixelio.de

More available books at **www.hansebooks.com**

THE COLONY

OF

BRITISH HONDURAS,

ITS RESOURCES AND PROSPECTS;

WITH PARTICULAR REFERENCE TO ITS INDIGENOUS PLANTS AND ECONOMIC PRODUCTIONS.

BY

D. MORRIS, M.A., F.L.S., F.G.S.,
Director of Public Gardens and Plantations, Jamaica.

LONDON:
EDWARD STANFORD, 55, CHARING CROSS.
1883.

[*All Rights Reserved.*]

LONDON:
HARRISON AND SONS, PRINTERS IN ORDINARY TO HER MAJESTY,
ST. MARTIN'S LANE.

PREFACE.

At the close of last year, at the invitation of the Government, I paid a short visit to the Colony of British Honduras.

The general results, as regards its flora and economic productions, are contained in the following pages. Owing to the facilities placed at my disposal, and the valuable assistance kindly accorded to me both officially and privately, I was enabled during my stay to travel over nearly one thousand miles of the country, and to see most of its salient features.

The account given of the indigenous plants of the colony is, however, by no means complete; indeed, in my anxiety to deal chiefly with those of economic value, I have omitted many of purely botanical interest, trusting that a systematic and exhaustive examination of the flora of British Honduras will, at no distant date, be undertaken under the auspices of Government. This little work, has, therefore, no pretensions, beyond being an attempt to give some account of the resources of the colony, and to supply a few practical hints to those who are, or about to be, engaged in developing them.

In England, little is known of British Honduras, and that little not of a very flattering character.

Its climate has been maligned, its resources only partially acknowledged, and the somewhat unsavoury reputation of Spanish Honduras has been extended to this little country, "which has afforded one of the most remarkable instances of British enterprise and energy."

Once the home of buccaneers, afterwards, for more than a hundred and fifty years, a mere station for cutting mahogany and logwood, its fortunes have practically been in the hands of a few monopolists. These, holding nearly all the land, have been content to get from it, in a lazy, desultory, and somewhat spasmodic manner, such timber and dyewoods as lay within reach of the principal rivers.

Now, however, such supplies are becoming exhausted, and as the land monopoly has been broken by the enforced sale of extensive tracts of forests, the colony enters practically upon a new phase of existence.

Its ultimate destiny will depend no less upon the wisdom and discretion of its rulers, than upon the character of the settlers likely to be attracted to it.

My object has been to place, in as clear and as impartial a manner as possible, the circumstances which at present obtain in the colony, and, starting from a consideration of its soil, climate, and vegetable productions, to indicate in what directions it is capable of being gradually developed and enriched. I am too deeply sensible of the results which usually follow the extensive and reckless cutting down of tropical forests, to advocate a wholesale denudation of crown lands in British Honduras. I trust, therefore, the question of retaining in permanent forest the chief watersheds of the country, as well as wooded belts in the neighbourhood of streams and springs, will receive the earnest and careful attention of the legislature.

With this important point well kept in view, I believe the Government would do well to offer every reasonable facility for the establishment of permanent plantations in the colony, and for attracting to it an intelligent race of planters, possessing the necessary capital and energy.

At present, several hundred thousand acres of some of the

finest lands to be found in any British dependency, produce an annual export value (in mahogany) of only £50,000. This sum is attained in Jamaica in the export value of such a "minor product" as oranges.

That the export value of oranges from Jamaica is equal to that of mahogany—the great staple industry of British Honduras—is a new and somewhat startling fact. It serves, however, to show what a change is gradually taking place in the development of the West India Islands by means of the fruit trade with America.

No other group of our Colonial possessions is, geographically, so favourably placed as the West Indies for the development of small industries. Within three days of New Orleans, and within seven days of New York, they may be termed the Channel Islands of the United States and Canada, supplying tropical fruits and raw tropical produce to a population numbering over fifty million souls. Within eighteen or twenty days of England and the Continent, they have markets for the larger and more permanent staples, placing them at any time independent of the States, and serving to keep up their connection with the mother country.

Wisely and generously regarded, the development of small industries, and especially the fruit trade in the West Indies, should lead, little by little, to the building up of a more wholesome as well as a more permanent prosperity, than anything which existed during the days of slavery.

The fruit trade has initiated a system of cash payment on the spot, which is fast extending to other industries; the result is, that the cultivator and the planter are placed at once in possession of means for continuing their cultural operations, and for extending them to their fullest extent. As a case in point, I may mention that the development of the fruit trade in

Jamaica is the means of circulating more than £150,000 annually amongst all classes of the community; and this large sum is immediately available, without the vexatious delays formerly experienced in establishing other and more permanent industries. Under the old system, the planter was for the most part in the hands of merchants and agents; he seldom had full control of his produce, and was so restricted in his selection of a market that he often suffered much thereby.

This new departure in the sale of West India produce is only beginning to be felt, but its ultimate effects will no doubt tend to such an emancipation of the planter, that these tropical lands will, in time, become as prosperous as they are beautiful and fair.

British Honduras, in these respects at least, will have a clear start. Its magnificent lands have hitherto been untouched, save to yield their rich store of timber and dyewoods; its planters will from the first have a convenient and abundant market for their produce, and by means of the sale of early maturing crops of fruits and vegetables, they will be able to work with a smaller capital, and maintain themselves free from the encumbrances which have hitherto been the bane of their brethren in the West India Islands.

In speaking so particularly of minor products in connection with British Honduras, I do not by any means wish it to be inferred that the larger industries are not likely to succeed there. Provided sufficient capital is available for the purpose, and the labour supply is guaranteed, there is no country where they could do better.

South of Belize River, and extending for many miles on each side of such rivers as the Rio Grande and others, there are extensive areas of fine land admirably suited for sugar-cane cultivation, where the *usine* system especially might be adopted with every prospect of success. Further inland, cacao plantations might cover hundreds of acres of fine, undulating country; while the finest coffee should flourish on the slopes and higher lands of the Cockscomb country, and along the western frontier.

For the general facts connected with British Honduras, I am indebted to official papers and reports published in the colony, as well as information kindly supplied to me by Mr. Fowler, the Colonial Secretary, Captain Marriner, Mr. A. Williamson, and others. To Captain Marriner, who accompanied me in my visit to the Southern Settlements, I was greatly indebted, and it is a source of great regret to me to find that, since I left the colony, this able officer has lost his life on the river Hondu.

To His Excellency, Colonel Sir Robert W. Harley, C.B., K.C.M.G., Lieutenant-Governor of British Honduras, I have to express thanks for much personal kindness and for generous hospitality.

For the drawing of the fruit of *Castilloa elastica,* and the design on the cover of this little work, I am indebted to my friend, Mrs. W. T. Thiselton-Dyer.

London, October 15th, 1883.

CONTENTS.

CHAPTER I.
PAGE

British Honduras. Position and neighbouring States. Historical Sketch. Constitution. Area. Boundaries. Coast-line. Interior. Highlands. River system. Belize. Chief institutions. Health. Harbour. Population. Imports, exports, and revenue. Chief industries. Minerals. Wild animals. Bird life. Fish. Turtle. Conchs. Snakes. Flies. Leaf-cutting ants 1

CHAPTER II.

Belize down the Coast. Sibun River. Manattee Bay. Mullin's River. Fruit Companies. Tracts of fine land. Communication by river impeded. Colston Point. North Stann Creek. Commerce Bight coco-nuts. All Pines. Regalia and Serpon sugar estates. Factory for extracting oil from cohune-nuts. Old saw-mills. Labour for sugar estates. Wages. Journey up Sittee River. Scenery and vegetation. Pit-pan travelling. Forest growth. Lands for bananas, coffee, cacao, oranges. Hell Gates. South Stann Creek. Monkey River. Spaniards. Creoles. Caribs. Walize Fruit Company. Point Ycacos. Deep River. Port Honduras. Seven Hills district. Sugar estate. Yield per acre. "Fly." Rio Grande River. Toledo Settlement. Ponta Gorda. Neat Carib village. Return to Belize.. .. 25

CHAPTER III.

Trip to western districts. Haul-over. Cramer's Bank. Bridge over Sibun Swamp. John Young's Pine-ridge. Camping out. Butcher Burn's Bank. Limestone Hills. Rich soils. Bush Travelling. Gale Creek. Bever Dam. Mahogany forest. Mahogany works. Castile Bank. Prickly bambu. Mount Pleasant. Bad roads. Orange Walk. Government lands for sale. How mahogany is cut. Trucking mahogany. Logwood cutting. Roaring Creek. Savannah Bank. Warree Head Creek. Monkey Fall Savannah. Granny Creek. Mount Hope. The Cayo. Coffee plantation. Position and importance of the Cayo. Communication with Belize. Indian settlement at San Francisco. To Belize by river in dory 40

B

CHAPTER IV.

Flora of British Honduras. First impressions of the country. Mangrove-trees. Characteristics of vegetation of the interior dependent on geological features. Underlying strata. How deposited. Geological floor. Glacial action. Icebergs. Reasons for adopting glacial theory. Pine-ridge country. Vegetation. Pine-trees, pimento-thatch, crabboe, haha. Distribution of pine-ridges. Use of pine-wood. White and yellow pine. Resin and turpentine from pine-trees. How to extract turpentine. Cohune-ridge. Cohune palm. Description: leaves, stem, and fruit. Cohune seeds. Oil. Timber-trees. Mahogany. Value of export. Common cedar. Logwood. Sapodilla. Santa Maria. Fiddle-wood. Rosewood. Salmwood. Braziletto. Ironwood. Mahoe. Numerous undetermined woods. Locust-tree. Cashaw. Edible candle-tree. Palms. Orchids. Ferns 53

CHAPTER V.

Cacao plant. *T. angustifolia*. Shade necessary. Socunusco or Tabasco cacao. Castilloa or Central American rubber. Description of tree: leaves, flowers, and fruit. How to collect seeds. How to raise plants. How to tap trees. How to prepare the rubber. Use of juice of the moon-plant. Use of alum. Preparation of rubber ready for shipment. Yield of trees. Value. Extended use of the Castilloa tree. Shade trees in general. Superiority of Castilloa over other shade trees. Ceara rubber-trees. Soil, situation, and districts for the Castilloa. Distance apart. Pruning. Returns of cultivated trees. Vanilla plant. Found wild and in bearing. Value. Directions for cultivation. How to fertilise flowers. How to cure beans. Fibre plants. Pita and henequin. How to establish a henequin plantation. Return at the end of five or six years. Preparation of fibre. Value of the industry in Yucatan. Cockspur-tree. Tococa. Habits of ants. Provision-tree. Indigo. Arnatto. Karamani, or hog-gum. Oil of Ben. Balsam of Tolu. Balsam of Copaiba. Guaco. Corkwood. Manchineel 72

CHAPTER VI.

Sugar-cane cultivation. Its introduction. Cost of production. Causes of decline of sugar industry. How to be revived. Muscavado sugar. New varieties of canes to be introduced. Banana cultivation. Hints to cultivators. Abundant land for bananas. Present position of the industry. Cacao. Advantages possessed by British Honduras. Nature of land. How to start a plantation. Shade plants required. India-rubber-tree. Liberian coffee. Market value in America. Topping and pruning. Pulping machines. Oranges, limes, and lemons. Coco-nuts: prolific yield. How to plant. Planting distances. Cost of plantations. Export trade. Rice. Indian corn. Tobacco. Pine-apples, how to cultivate. Cinchona 89

CHAPTER VII.

Nutmegs. Soil and situation. Rainfall. Curing of nutmegs and mace. Yield of trees. Pimento or allspice. Cinnamon and camphor. Cardamoms. Elevation, soil, and shade. Returns per acre. Black pepper. Native peppers. Ipecacuanha: true and bastard. Variety from Carthagena. Ginger. Turmeric. Sarsaparilla. How cultivated in Jamaica. Returns per acre. Oil plants. Wanglo, pindar, castor-oil, palm-oil, and oil of Ben. Cloves. Fodder plants. Guinea grass. Para or water grass. Bahama grass. Natural grasses of the country. Rain-tree. Fodder and shade. Fruit-trees. Mango. Bread-fruit. Star-apple. Akee and Avocado pear. Mangosteen. Durian and new fruit-trees. Food plants. Yams, sweet potatoes, beans, and cassava. Pumpkins, cucumbers, and melons. Vegetables and salads 104

CHAPTER VIII.

Labour question. Indigenous labour: how to improve. Masters and Servants Act. Carib. Indian. Cooly immigration. Views of Sir Frederick Barlee. Advance and Truck systems. Local enterprise. Crown lands. Conditions of sale. Navigable rivers. Steam communication with New Orleans, New York, and London. Railways. Agricultural Board. Botanic Gardens. Importation and distribution of seeds and plants. Geological Survey. Climate of British Honduras. Meteorological observations. Price of food. House-rent. Horses. Currency. Religion. Education. Hints to intending settlers 117

APPENDIX 144

INDEX 147

THE COLONY OF BRITISH HONDURAS.

CHAPTER I.

British Honduras. Position and neighbouring States. Historical sketch. Constitution. Area. Boundaries. Coast-line. Interior. Highlands. River system. Belize. Chief institutions. Health. Harbour. Population. Imports, exports, and revenue. Chief industries. Minerals. Wild animals. Bird life. Fish. Turtle. Conchs. Snakes. Flies. Leaf-cutting ants.

FOR the stay-at-home Briton, no less than for the tropical traveller, it may be pardonable to mention that the Colony of British Honduras occupies a small portion of the Atlantic slope of Central America. It is situated immediately to the south of the Mexican State of Yucatan, and has, as near neighbours, the Republican States of Guatemala, Salvadora, and that of the Mosquito Coast, or Spanish Honduras.

It is the only portion of the mainland of Central America where the British flag flies; and hence, in a political sense, it has been regarded as an oasis of freedom and right, amidst successive outbursts of rebellion and strife, which, unhappily, too often characterises these Republics.

British Honduras began, some two hundred years ago, as a logwood and mahogany-cutting settlement; the pioneers, at that time, apparently having no intention to make a permanent occupation there. From the beginning, Spain regarded the settlement as an infringement of her sovereign rights; the Indians resented an invasion of their lands, and made periodical raids upon the mahogany works and stores; while it has been reserved to the United States to regard the existence of this British Colony, "which was in existence more than a century before the Great Republic was dreamt of, as an infringement of the *ex poste facto* doctrine, associated with the name of President Monroe." Happily, however, Spain has wholly ceded her rights; Guatemala, by the treaty of 1859, has agreed to the main boundary line of the interior; Mexico, by a treaty of 1816, and a further recognition in 1852, has accepted the *status quo;* while the Clayton-Bulwer treaty of 1859 has fairly exempted the Colony of British Honduras from all operations of the Monroe doctrine.

To give a brief historical sketch, it may be added that Honduras was discovered in 1502 by Columbus, and in 1518 Grijalva landed on the Island of Cozumel, and named the country New Spain. In 1638, a few British subjects first inhabited Honduras, having been wrecked on the coast; and in 1642 the English took possession of the Island of Ruatan. Campeachy was attacked and taken by a few English sailors in 1659. Logwood cutters settled in 1662 at Cape Catoche. The Treaty of Madrid, 1667, stipulated that six months' notice should be given by either party, in case of war, to give time to parties to remove their merchandise and effects. In July, 1670, Spain ceded, in perpetuity to Great Britain, by treaty, with plenary right of sovereignty, all lands in the West Indies, or in any part of America held by the English at the time (Art. vii). Logwood establishments increased rapidly from this date, the population of the settlement amounted to 700 white settlers, among whom was the famous Admiral Benbow, and a creek on which he worked bears his name to this day.

Commissioners for the Government of Honduras were first appointed 31st July, 1745.

The Treaty of Paris, 1763, required all fortifications in the Bay of Honduras to be demolished, the right of cutting logwood was recognised, but plantations or manufactures forbidden. The Spaniards immediately after signing the treaty, drove the cutters from Rio Hondu, which called forth the disclaimer published in the *London Gazette*, 21st July, 1764. The King, in 1765, gave a " constitution to the people," founded on their ancient customs, viz., "legislating by public meetings, and the election of magistrates annually by the free suffrage of the people." This, it may be remarked, was the freest constitution ever enjoyed by, or granted to, a British settlement.

Sir William Burnaby was sent to the settlement to make the necessary arrangements, and the inhabitants were then put in full possession of their lands and rights. Captain Cook, the celebrated navigator, accompanied Sir William Burnaby, and they codified the laws and customs of the settlement, which were afterwards published and known as Burnaby's laws.

From 1779 to June, 1784, the settlement was hardly in existence, almost everything having been destroyed by the Spaniards.

The Treaty of Peace at Versailles, 3rd September, 1783, restored the settlement, and allowed the right of cutting logwood between the Belize and Rio Hondu rivers, but the Baymen were still debarred from making plantations : and Spanish Commissioners were to visit the settlement twice annually to see if the provisions of the treaty were fulfilled. This treaty apparently waived the rights secured by Article vii of the Treaty of 1670, for the sovereignty of the Spanish Crown is distinctly recognised; and in 1786 a Superintendent was appointed on a memorial from the settlers.

On the 27th May, 1784, Don Zevallez, Governor of Yucatan, " commissioned by the Court of Spain to make a formal delivery to the British nation of the lands allotted for the cutting of logwood, delivered the same to the English Commissioners at the mouth of the New River, agreeable to map and instructions received from his sovereign—having given over the boundaries and placed the proper marks and trees on the land side, as well as executed every necessary formality for the purpose."

Additional articles to the Treaty of 1783 were made in 1786 at a convention held in London, whereby the right of cutting mahogany was formally granted, and the Mosquito Coast abandoned. The settlers from there joined the Belize settlement, 1787. Since the invasion of 1798, when the Spaniards were repulsed, the English have held the territory by right of conquest in addition to claims of occupation.

In 1819, the Criminal Court was established by Act of Parliament, and Her Majesty's Superintendent was appointed for the first time under Royal Letters Patent.

An Executive Council was appointed in 1839 to assist the Superintendent.

In 1850, the inhabitants petitioned for a change in the system of government.

The Act of 1853 reformed and amended the ancient system of government, and it constituted a legislative body, consisting of eighteen elected and three nominated members. The settlement gradually grew into a recognised colony, and was so officially proclaimed on 12th May, 1862, when a Lieutenant-Governor was appointed in lieu of a Superintendent. The reformed constitution, after the usual variety of struggles incident to mixed communities, became unworkable, and the ancient institutions of the settlement drifted into the form of a Crown Colony Government, the old elective assembly committing suicide in 1870.

The present constitution of the colony is regulated by a local

Act of 1870. By this enactment, a Legislative Council is established, consisting of five official, and not less than four unofficial members, to be named by the Queen, or provisionally appointed by the Lieutenant-Governor, subject to Her Majesty's approval. The official members are: the Chief Justice, the Colonial Secretary, the Senior Military Officer (if of or above the rank of Major), the Treasurer, and the Attorney-General. The Lieutenant-Governor is President of the Council.

There is also an Executive or Privy Council, consisting of the Senior Military Officer, the Colonial Secretary, the Treasurer, and the Attorney-General. (If below the rank of Major, the Senior Military Officer ranks last.)

British Honduras has a sea-board, extending almost due north and south, of about 160 miles; it contains an estimated area of about 7,500 square miles. Thus the colony is about one-third the size of England; nearly twice the size of Jamaica; and almost equal to the whole of the British West India Islands put together.

The boundaries of the colony are defined by the river Hondu and Yucatan on the north; by a straight line drawn from the rapids of Gracias á Dios on the river Sarstoon to Garbutt's Falls on the river Belize, thence due north to the Mexican frontier, on the west; by a portion of Guatemala with the Sarstoon River on the south; while the Bay of Honduras and the Caribbean Sea are to the east.

Along the whole of the coast, and extending for many miles to the eastward, are numerous coral islands, or cays, some of which are simply covered with mangrove-trees, whilst others are under partial cultivation. The largest of these coral islands is Turneffe (Terra Nova), lying about 30 miles from Belize, composed of numerous mangrove cays and lagoons, with here and there passages for boats. To the extreme east there are

Northern Two Cays, Saddle Cay, Hot Cay, and Half-Moon Cay: the latter, about 80 miles from Belize, has a lighthouse which gives the first intimation of the coast. Another important light is on English Cay about half-way between the southern point of Turneffe and Belize. Between Turneffe and the mainland are numerous small cays, some of which are only just visible, rendering the navigation difficult, if not dangerous. About eight miles north-east of Belize is St. George's Cay, a small island affording good sea-bathing, and, being well exposed to the inspiriting influences of the trade-winds, is utilised by the inhabitants of Belize as a sanatorium. To the south, the whole coast-line is fringed by numberless coral islets upon which the surf breaks with considerable force, leaving the inner waters, however, comparatively calm. The total area of the cays is estimated at 212 square miles.

The most northern, and next to Belize the most important, town in the colony is Corosal, situated near the mouth of the New River, and a *depôt* for all the mahogany and logwood cut on its banks, as well as of those on the river Hondu. The coast-line from Corosal to Belize, after running due east as far as Rocky Point, turns suddenly to the southward, with a portion of Yucatan and Ambergris Cay between it and the open sea. After passing Hicks Cay and the Hen and Chickens Cay, the principal mouth of the Belize River is passed, the smaller and more southerly mouth being that on which the town of Belize stands. On the headland, near the latter, is Fort George, built in 1803, as a defence to the settlement.

To the south of Belize, every river mouth or "bar" is the scene of a settlement or small village: many of which, however, consist merely of a few huts.

The country generally near the coast is low and only slightly raised above the sea. In the interior, however, it is

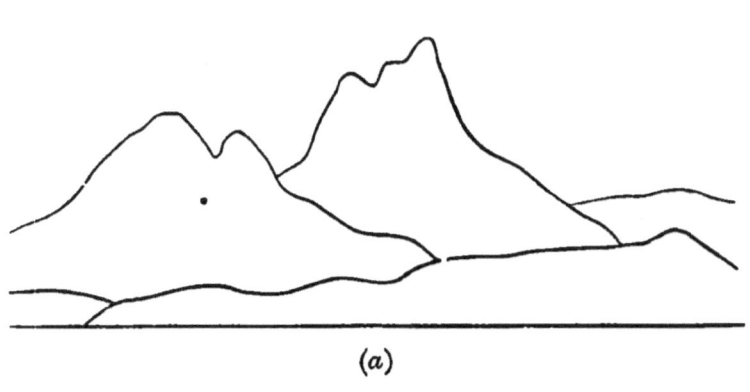

(a)

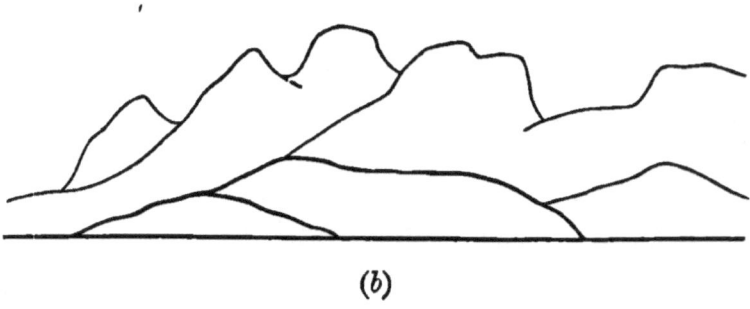

(b)

OUTLINE SKETCH OF THE COCKSCOMB MOUNTAINS, BRITISH HONDURAS.
(HIGHEST PEAK ABOUT 4,000 FEET.)

(a) As seen from Serpon Sugar Estate, near All Pines.
(b) As seen from the sea off Point Placentia. The low coast ranges in the foreground.

greatly diversified, especially in the south, where hilly or undulating country runs almost close to the sea-coast.

The general impressions of Europeans respecting British Honduras being derived from the town of Belize, they are apt to conclude that the whole country is nothing but a swamp, and that the climate " is only second to that of the pestilential coast of Western Africa." This estimate is as fair to British Honduras as if the Plaistow Marshes were taken as typical of England, or the Gulf Coast as typical of the United States. Being a continental element, and lying between 16° and 18° north latitude, the mean annual temperature is much lower than is usually supposed. Again, the trade-winds sweeping uninterruptedly over it, clear away all miasmic influences, and keep the air pure and comparatively cool.

The chief highlands of the colony are situated towards the western frontier, being composed of spurs and ridges connected with the chief mountain zone of Central America. In the northern part of the colony there are only isolated ridges and domes, seldom more than about 200 feet or 300 feet high. To the south of the Belize River, the spurs and ridges from the central range strike obliquely across the colony, being very abundant in bold, craggy hills at the head-waters of the Sibun, Manattee, and Mullin's Rivers, until they culminate in the extensive slopes and high peaks of the Cockscomb Mountains. These mountains, rising to a height of 4,000 feet, are only about 40 miles in a direct line from the coast: and from the extent of country covered by them, as well as from their picturesque outline, especially as seen at sunset from the sea, they fully redeem the colony from the imputation of flatness so often brought against it. This country to the south of the Belize River, comprising fully one-half of the colony, has until lately been marked in most maps as " unexplored territory: query inhabited." But owing to the energy and enterprise of Mr. Fowler, Colonial Secretary, it has been recently traversed by a small party of Europeans, led by himself, who, accompanied by Indian carriers, accomplished the entire journey from Garbutt's Falls, on the Old River, to the sea-coast at Deep River, in about a month. The results of the expedition are thus tersely summed up by Mr. Fowler:—

"The interior of the colony was found to be a succession of valleys and hills, from 1,200 feet to 3,300 feet above the level of the sea, and may be divided into pastoral, mineral, and agricultural districts, each of which can be fairly defined. That it was once inhabited is proved by the ancient ruins found during the journey, and population is only requisite to convert a desolate waste into luxuriant homes, for the soil is rich. The climate would be found suitable to Europeans, and the wide range of latitude might easily be availed of as circumstances required."

The river system of the colony is a very extensive one, and it is chiefly owing to its rivers, which have afforded natural highways to the interior, that the country has been so far developed. The two chief rivers in the north are the Hondu and the New Rivers. These both rise in the neighbourhood of lands towards the western frontier, in the latitude of Belize, and flow along parallel depressions in a north-easterly direction, emptying themselves into the large estuarine expansion of the Hondu. The New River is chiefly fed by the waters of the New River lagoon and Crab-catch lagoon. On its banks are several large mahogany works, as also the settlement and military station of Orange Walk, about 30 miles distant from Corosal. The most important, as well as the richest river valley in the colony is that of the Old River, sometimes called the Belize River. Its total length, from the town of Belize to the western frontier, cannot be less than 100 miles, while one at least of its tributaries rises in the Republic of Guatemala. At the junction of its branches, near the frontier, is the small settlement, called the Cayo, which, as being the nearest station in British territory to Guatemala, is likely to become a place of considerable importance. Pit-pans, or shallow river boats, can pass from Belize to the Cayo, and often by these means English goods of considerable value are brought up and supplied to Peten and other places across the frontier.

The upper portions of the valley of the Belize River widen into broad expanses of rich fertile plains, some 30 or 40 miles across.

Along the whole course of the Belize River there are numerous mahogany works, or "banks," where logs are collected and trimmed before being despatched to the *depôt* at Belize. Next to the Cayo, Orange Walk (Old River) is the most important settlement. Here, and generally in the upper portions of the river, the banks on both sides are very high and generally covered with umbrageous figs, the fine-leaved prickly bamboo (*Guadua*), or tall, rank-growing sedges and canes. Close to the water's edge is a beautiful white-flowered *Pancratium*, or Caribbean lily. At Never Delay the banks are about 40 feet high, composed of a yellowish clay. At Rock Dondo is a huge mass of porous limestone in the middle of the river; and a little below, at Middle Station, are the upper rapids or falls which restrict the navigation to craft drawing only a few inches of water. The "Big Falls," a little lower down, during certain seasons, are rather formidable rapids, which require the utmost care on the part of loaded pit-pans to pass safely up and down. "Two-headed Cabbage" is the name of a landing, supposed to have been given on account of a cabbage palm having developed a branching stem, an anomaly which occurs somewhat rarely amongst coco-nut palms. All along the banks of this river numerous settlements are dotted about, the people evidently looking upon it as their natural highway to the coast, as well as their only means of procuring supplies. Below Bakers is a small church, raised, as are most of the houses, on piles or pillars so as to be out of reach of floods. The congregation in this instance, being mostly river people, must come to service from far and near, in boats. Just above Boom, where the mahogany logs are stopped in their passage down the river, and claimed by their several owners, there is a fine specimen of what is called a royal marriage, amongst plants, namely, the stem of a palm invested or embraced by that of a fig. The latter, starting probably as a small seedling, amongst the vegetable matter accumulated at the bases of the fronds of the palm, in process of time grows, by means of its aerial roots, into a large tree, almost entirely covering the stem of the latter. The fig sends out, as it grows, numerous large, widespreading branches, while the palm, whose stem is now completely invested by the fig, continues to grow also, until at last a kind of composite plant is seen, partly a fig, and partly a palm. The latter, however, as a rule, rises above the fig, and is seen spreading its magnificent fronds, quivering and glancing in the bright sunshine.

Some few miles below the Boom, the river divides into two branches: one goes out directly towards the east to the sea, whereas the other takes a sharp turn to the southward, and passes through the town of Belize. Belize was, no doubt, in the first instance, selected as the headquarters of the settlement, owing to its position at the mouth of the principal river. It certainly could not have possessed any other advantages.

Belize, the capital of British Honduras, is situated on one of the mouths of the Old River, near Fort George, and occupies a position on both sides of it. The name of Belize is supposed to be a Spanish corruption of Wallace, the name of a Scotchman, a noted pirate. Or, possibly, it may be derived from the French *balise*, a beacon, which might have been erected to warn mariners of the abode of pirates. The town is practically cut off from the interior by numerous lagoons, one of which, however, is now bridged. The site of the town is somewhat facetiously described as composed of mahogany chips, and sand dredged out of the harbour. Be that as it may, the town is one of the brightest and cleanest in the West Indies, and although small, is the seat of an extensive trade, not only with the settlements in the colony itself, but with all the neighbouring Republics. The population in 1881 was about 10,000, consisting chiefly of Europeans (amongst which Scotch predominate), Negroes, Creoles, Spaniards, and a few Indians.

Belize is the seat of Government, and possesses several public buildings, the chief and most striking of which is the new Court House, occupying a central position, and having the Government offices below. The Lieutenant-Governor's residence, built in 1814, occupies a commanding position at one extremity of the town, to the south; and following the contour of the harbour, and facing the sea, are numerous stores and residences, which, shaded by coco-nuts and tropical trees, present a very picturesque appearance. Owing to the dangers arising from fires, all the buildings are roofed with iron, and lined with felt. The two portions of the town are connected by a bridge, under which there is a continual flow of traffic in mahogany, logwood, and pit-pans loaded with goods, starting on their long journey— some 100 miles—for the Cayo, on the western frontier. The chief institutions of the town are the public hospital, maintained solely by Government, and with accommodation for thirty-six patients; the lunatic asylum, with accommodation for thirty patients; the poor-house, with accommodation for thirty-six patients; and the common gaol, with about seventy inmates.

All these are under excellent management and control, and reflect great credit on the officers in charge. The military quarters and buildings are to the north of the town, where they have the full benefit of the cool sea-breezes. There is a good hotel in the town, with extensive accommodation of a superior character.

The houses are mostly surrounded by patches of garden, with some fruit and shade-trees. Owing to the sandy nature of the soil, which is impregnated with salt, and the proximity of water to the surface, gardening in Belize is pursued under very disadvantageous circumstances. Crabs dig up and destroy many plants; while rats, attracted by the presence of coco-nuts, are very destructive to bulbs and roots. The Oleander thrives luxuriantly everywhere. The mignonette-tree, or henna-plant (*Lawsonia inermis*), gives the air a delicious fragrance at night; while the flamboyante, with its masses of scarlet flowers, the allamanda, the temple-flower (*Plumeria alba*), and numerous ixoras brighten up and cheer what would otherwise be a mere waste of sand and bahama-grass. Many fine specimens of the royal palm of Cuba (*Oreodoxa regia*) grow in the town gardens, as also *Livistonas* and thatch-palm (*Thrinax*). The chief feature, however, in the landscape is the coco-nut palm, which, with its widespreading fronds rattling in the sea-breeze, grows luxuriantly everywhere.

From its position and surroundings, Belize might naturally be looked upon as a very unhealthy town. Surrounded for the most part by mangrove swamps, with perfectly level country extending for many miles to the interior, and without any system of drainage, except what the sandy soil and the harbour afford, it would appear to possess all the elements of unhealthiness. From actual experience and very careful returns, however, the health of Belize is proved to be exceptionally good; the death rate (33·0 per 1,000) being below that of Dublin, and only slightly in excess of that of Paris and New York.

The healthiness of Belize, and of the country generally, as Mr. Belt noticed with regard to Greytown, is no doubt due to what appears at first sight an element of danger, viz., the perfect flatness of the ground. "Where there are hills, there must be hollows, and in these the air stagnates; whilst here, where the land is quite level, the trade-winds that blow pretty constantly find their way to every part, and carry off the emanations of the soil." Many instances could be given of other towns similarly situated, possessing what may be termed a healthy climate, for the tropics, and evidently arising from the same causes.

The harbour of Belize is approached by a somewhat intricate passage, amongst the coral reefs, which abound in the offing; but it is generally well sheltered, and has a secure anchorage. A project is in contemplation to extend and improve the harbour by erecting a pier and tramway in accordance with suggestions made by Mr. Siccama, sent out specially for the purpose, and subsequently approved by the Secretary of State. Should these improvements be carried out, Belize will become an important port in this part of the world, and greatly extend the commercial interests of the mother country amongst the Central and South American Republics.

The total population of the colony in 1881 was 27,452. Of this number 375, or less than 2 per cent., were returned as white, and 27,077 as coloured or black.

The Europeans, for the most part, are described as birds of passage, business or duty calling them there for a time; and very few appear to have entertained the thought of making permanent homes in the colony. Some American (white) settlers in the south are, however, an exception. The bulk of the inhabitants known as Belize Creoles are negroes, no doubt originally derived from the West Indian Islands. They are described as of excellent physique, and capable of great exertion in the laborious work of mahogany and logwood cutting. An attempt was made some years ago to introduce Chinese to supplement the labour demands of the colony, but, strange to say, they deserted *en masse* to the Santa Cruz Indians, who, although they declare extermination to "los blancos," have fraternised freely with the Chinamen. After the Creole element, possibly the Spaniard comes next. There is here, also, a large admixture of Spanish and Indian blood, with the usual result, of the worst features of both races being emphasised in their descendants. The other elements are Carib and pure Indian. The former is a fine quiet type of Indian: very skilful as a sailor, but not a good cultivator. The Indian pure and simple lives chiefly in the backwoods, and seldom troubles the white man, except when, during the occasional raids of Indians beyond the border, he is an object of suspicion and dread to the white population.

The total value of the imports, consisting of cigars, malt liquors, spirits, sugar (refined), tea, tobacco, wines, and general merchandise was £201,811. The total value of the exports, consisting chiefly of sugar, rum, mahogany, cedar, logwood, rosewood, fustic, ziricote, indiarubber, sarsaparilla, turtle, coco-nuts, bananas, and other fruits, was £247,403. The chief import trade of the country, amounting to about two-thirds, is with the United Kingdom; the next largest share is with the United States; while the remainder is divided amongst Mexico, Jamaica, and the Central American States. The chief export trade in timber and indiarubber is also with the United Kingdom, while the trade in coco-nuts and fresh fruits is almost entirely confined to the United States.

The annual revenue is £43,642, with no public debt.

CHIEF INDUSTRIES.

The chief industry of the colony is wood-cutting. The average annual export of mahogany is about three million feet, and of logwood about fifteen thousand tons. The cost of the former ready for shipment is from £8 to £10 per thousand feet, and of the latter from £2 to £3 per ton.

Wood-cutting operations have now been carried on for more than 200 years, and as a result much of the finest timber within easy reach of the principal rivers and their creeks has been cut down. There is, however, much fine timber still to be found in the interior, but probably beyond the reach of rivers. Hence it is believed that the construction of a railway will not only advance other industries, but at the same time stimulate the production and export of the old staples of the colony.

Out of an estimated extent of 1,280,000 acres of fine "cohune ridge," or alluvial virgin soil, in British Honduras, only some 10,000 acres, or less than one-hundredth part, is, or has been, under cultivation.

The cultivation of fruit for the American market has lately been started in consequence of steam communication having been regularly established under contract with New Orleans. Bananas, plantains, and coco-nuts are, so far, the staple articles of export, the prices obtained being 1s. 9d. to 2s. per bunch for bananas; 3s. to 4s. per 100 for plantains; and 70s. to 100s. per thousand for coco-nuts.

Much of the spirit of enterprise which has been developed in British Honduras during the last five years is no doubt due to the late Governor, now Sir Frederick P. Barlee, K.C.M.G., who endeavoured to create new industries, afforded facilities for the acquisition of Crown lands, and promoted the establishment of regular steam communication with New Orleans. At the present time, for experienced planters, who have already lived in tropical countries, and especially in the East, British

Honduras offers inducements superior, I believe, to those of most British Colonies. There are thousands of acres of magnificent land offered by Government at an upset price of a dollar an acre, capable of growing nearly every tropical product. Some of these lands are either near the banks of rivers, with easy communication with the coast, or on the coast itself. There is an abundant market for bananas, plantains, coco-nuts, oranges, pine-apples, and all tropical fruits in demand in America, and regular direct communication, by means of mail and other steamers, with both England and the States. For the cultivation of sugar-cane, coffee, tea, cacao, spices, tobacco, vanilla, and rice, British Honduras offers special advantages.

As regards mineral wealth, there has always existed an idea in the colony, suggested no doubt by the yield of mines in the neighbouring Republics, that precious stones, and especially gold, might be found in British Honduras. About five years ago this idea took a definite form, and steps were taken to explore the country at the head-waters of the Sittee River, and if possible find whether gold-bearing quartz existed there, and in the Cockscomb Mountains. The leaders of the party, accompanied by four Creoles, proceeded up the Sittee River, took the left branch, and found chiefly rocks of "blue and red slate, flint shingle and limestone." Finding the prospect in this direction so uninviting they retraced their steps, and then proceeded up the Main River. Taking a land journey to the westward, they found the country very broken and rugged: "a succession of steep hills and gulches" rendering travelling exceedingly laborious. No indications of minerals were met with, except occasionally huge quartz boulders in the bed of the river. Many valuable woods, such as Santa Maria, were found in abundance; but animal life was almost entirely absent, except in the coast-belt. After a month's absence in the bush the party at last was compelled to return to Belize fruitless. As a bald, inaccessible range of hills, running north and south, had been noticed at the back of the Cockscombs, it was determined to organise a second party and approach these hills from the neighbourhood of Garbutt's Falls, striking across country in a south-easterly course. This time the party was joined by Mr. Fowler, and an account of the expedition has been given by him in a very graphic and interesting manner.* In one locality a large quartz reef was found, forming the top of a ridge, and in some places projecting some 20 feet from the ground. Some pieces of this quartz, on being analysed in Belize, were pronounced to be gold-bearing quartz. In another district volcanic rock was frequently noticed, running in dykes due north and south. "It was very hard, and composed of all kinds of small pieces of rock, conglomerated into a solid mass, throughout which quartz was dispersed." Strong indications of minerals and many specimens of ore were also found in the neighbourhood of Deep River. Although no actual gold was found in this expedition, the formation of the country justified the belief that it is highly probable coal, gold, or silver may ultimately be found. The most promising mineral district is evidently a belt of country 20 or 30 miles broad, running north-east, and south-west from the south of the Cockscomb range, into the neighbouring Republics of Guatemala and Honduras, and parallel to, and distant from, the coast, as the crow flies, about 25 miles.

If the mines in the neighbouring countries were first studied, and the nature of the gold-bearing rocks there determined, the presence of such rocks in British Honduras would then be

---

* A narrative of a journey across the unexplored portion of British Honduras, with a sketch of the history and resources of the Colony, by Henry Fowler, Colonial Secretary. The Government Press, Belize, 1879.

simply a matter of observation. If, as will be suggested in a later chapter, a geological survey of the colony is organised, on the same lines as those so exhaustively and so efficiently carried out in Jamaica, Trinidad, and British Guiana, there is no doubt that its true mineral wealth would then be clearly indicated. So far, there are, apparently, some good grounds for belief in the existence of gold in the quartzy reefs of the Cockscomb country. And in other rocks, especially in the neighbourhood of those of volcanic origin, precious stones and fine crystals may not improbably be found. I have in my possession fine specimens of jaspar and other stones, picked up in the rivers of the colony, which have been much admired; and I have no doubt, if the sources of these rivers were systematically explored, much valuable information would be obtained.

For the agriculturist, the vast deposits of limestone are of interest as likely to yield good lime; and the numerous caves and caverns might yield largely bat manure, rich in ammonia and nitrogenous compounds invaluable for sugar-cane. The numerous cays might also be examined for guano and phosphates, which, instead of being exported to other countries, might render the cultivated lands of the colony most productive and remunerative. Fine building stone and marbles of great beauty are found in numerous sections along the southern rivers, and these will doubtless be utilised as the country becomes more developed and settled. Of wild animals, British Honduras possesses the puma, or Central American lion; the jaguar, or tiger; the ocelot, or spotted tiger-cat; the coyote, a small, wolf-like fox; the peccary, of which there are two kinds—the peccary proper, and the white-lipped peccary, or "warree," both formidable animals when met in droves. It is said that the jaguar will never attack warrees when packed, but looks out for the hindermost on a run, or a straggler. The warree has a small hole on the back, over the loin, which emits so powerful an odour that the presence of the animal can be detected at a considerable distance. When a warree is killed, the Indians immediately cut out this hole, and generally cure the meat by drying it in the sun, thus obtaining what is termed "barbecued pork." The tusks of the warree are very formidable weapons: as sharp as lancets. I was fortunate enough to see a tame warree in the neighbourhood of Orange Walk (Old River), kept by an old hunter; as also to obtain fine specimens of tusks. A small racoon was met in the neighbourhood of Mount Hope, which was killed while attacking the poultry of my host during the night. Other animals found in the colony are red deer, tapir or mountain cow, the iguana, small ant-eater, the quash, armadillo, squirrel, gibonet, and conies. The latter are usually termed rabbits. Alligators of large size infest most of the inland lagoons, and afford good sport at the out-stations. Of monkeys there are evidently several species. The baboons make most dismal sounds in the forests: their tones and howls being demoniacal. Along the coast the manatee is said to be occasionally seen, although becoming more and more rare with the attacks made upon it.

Of bird life, there is an abundance in most parts of the colony. The wild turkey, one of the most handsome birds in the world, is met with, but very rarely, on the western frontier, whence I believe a pair was lately sent to the Zoological Gardens, London. The domesticated turkey is raised in great abundance everywhere in the colony: the birds appear to be particularly strong and healthy here; and free from many of the diseases which attack them elsewhere. The curassow, the royal bird of Guatemala, is as large as a turkey, and, as seen in the forest, reminds one of the wild pea-fowl of the East Indies. The male bird is black, with yellow on the side of the head and throat; the female has a dull plumage, mostly brown speckled with white; both sexes have a full crest on the head, which they erect and move at pleasure. Other birds are white egrets, *Trogon*, toucans with monstrous bills, the quam, whistling ducks, partridges, wild pigeons, &c. Parrots are very plentiful; the most prized for talking are the yellow-headed parrots, obtained from Monkey River and places south. Of raptorial birds, the eagle, the "John-crow," or vulture, the osprey and hawk are well represented.

The sea, as well as the rivers, afford an abundant supply of excellent fish. As in the West Indies, the most prized are the callipever, snapper, bass, mullet, grooper, and king or june-fish. In the rivers, the mountain mullet, or tropical trout, affords not only good sport, but is most delicate eating.

Turtle is found along the coast, and during the season turtle-fishing is an established industry. The green-turtle is in chief request for food, the hawksbill and loggerhead being taken for the sake of the shell. Several fresh-water tortoises are found in the rivers and used for food, the chief being the "hiccatee."

The king, queen, and common conch are found in the outer cays and along shore, and the flesh of some used for food. It is very probable that, as in the Bahamas, the shells of these might form an important article of export, as they are largely used for cameos; and in the common conch is found a beautiful pale-pink pearl of great value. The value of shells exported from Bahamas is placed at £1,200 per annum, and of pearls at £3,000 per annum. A fine set of exhibits of these articles were lately shown at the International Fisheries Exhibition in London.

Of snakes, probably British Honduras has its share, in common with most tropical countries. The number of these which are venomous is much smaller, I believe, than is generally supposed. Those which are known to be venomous are the rattlesnake, the tommy-goff, or tamagasa, and the coral snake. The bite of the two former causes death in a few hours; but that of the latter, it is said, almost directly. In Mr. Fowler's trip across the country he reports having killed seven "poisonous brutes" during the journey. "A snake locally known as the 'jumping tommy-goff' was the principal and most dangerous specimen encountered; but one large black snake, about 3 feet long, with a grey, flat head, was killed, which none of us recognised."

There is a beautiful grass-green-coloured snake, known as the whip snake, which is probably not venomous.

Scorpions, especially the small brown-coloured species common in the West Indies, are plentiful, as also the tarantula spider, which is greatly feared.

Of "flies," mosquitoes and sand-flies are as abundant on the coast as in any country similarly situated: though perhaps not more troublesome than in Florida and many places infested by them. In the interior, except at certain seasons of the year, they are not troublesome in open places. One pest, which I have met nowhere else, is found during certain seasons of the year in low moist districts, which the natives call the "botlass" fly. This is a small black fly, shaped somewhat like a bottle—hence its name—which is only found in the daytime, but whose bite on the hands and face is most troublesome, if not indeed venomous. Its sting leaves a black mark, surrounded by a small reddish-coloured area, which does not disappear until the skin is worn off. "During flood times the natives living in their midst are obliged to shut themselves up in their houses, and stop every aperture to keep out the flies." While in the upper lands on the Mullin's River, rubber-gathering, I made the acquaintance of these pests, which certainly, in persistence and severity, can be compared to nothing except the land-leeches of the East Indies, or the grass-lice (ticks) of Brazil.

The leaf-cutting ant, or "wevey" (*Œcodoma*), is a familiar object in the forests, where its crowded and well-worn paths cross and recross in all directions. This ant, so graphically described by Mr. Belt, is a pest of no mean importance in the colony, since, if not checked, it will soon destroy a plantation of coffee, cacao, orange, or indeed anything in its vicinity. By its ceaseless attacks upon the leaves of yams and fruit-trees, the natives are often debarred from extending their small plots of garden ground; but as shown, in more than one instance, its ravages are easily checked if the nest is discovered and treated either with boiling water, a solution of carbolic acid, or anything of a virulent nature. The carbolic acid in the proportion of one pint to four buckets of water, after being well stirred, should be poured down the burrows. Within a short time the nest is entirely abandoned, and if the ants are not altogether destroyed, they move away in a wholesale migration to a considerable distance, and seldom revisit the spot again.

Having thus far given a general sketch and description of the colony, I will now proceed to give an account of the places visited by me, and of the chief points, connected with the economic plants and resources of the country, which came under notice.

CHAPTER II.

Belize down the Coast. Sibun River. Manattee Bay. Mullin's River. Fruit Companies. Tracts of fine land. Communication by river impeded. Colston Point. North Stann Creek. Commerce Bight coco-nuts. All Pines. Regalia and Serpon sugar estates. Factory for extracting oil from cohune-nuts. Old saw-mills. Labour for sugar estates. Wages. Journey up Sittee River. Scenery and vegetation. Pit-pan travelling. Forest growth. Lands for bananas, coffee, cacao, oranges. Hell Gates. South Stann Creek. Monkey River. Spaniards. Creoles. Caribs. Walize Fruit Company. Point Ycacos. Deep River. Port Honduras. Seven Hills district. Sugar estate. Yield per acre. "Fly." Rio Grande River. Toledo Settlement. Ponta Gorda. Neat Carib village. Return to Belize.

WITH the approval of Government, it was decided to visit first the settlements to the south of Belize, which were all within convenient reach by sea and river communication. A small schooner, the "Telegraph," was engaged; and, in company with Captain Marriner, Inspector of Police, we left Belize on the morning of the 15th November.

On account of the numerous reefs which fringe the coast, and run almost parallel to it, at distances varying from 10 to 15 miles, the water within is so sheltered that it is generally suitable for navigation by even the smallest boats. These often travel distances of 150 to 200 miles along the coast, carrying produce to Belize and taking back English and American goods to the settlements. A good run down the coast, past the mouth of the Sibun River and Manattee Bay, brought us, early the next morning, off the mouth of Mullin's River. Near Manattee Bay, the Manattee Fruit Company has opened land under favourable circumstances. Having landed at Mullin's River we walked through the village, at the bar, and for some distance along the shore under the shade of coco-nut palms. On the upper portions of the Mullin's River there are two small plantations, established for the cultivation of fruit, viz., the British Honduras Fruit Company and the Belize Fruit Company, each with a capital of $5,000. As in most instances along the coast, the land within easy reach of the village had already been under cultivation by the natives, and consequently to obtain the finest stretches of virgin forest, it is necessary to go some distance up the river. The Mullin's River is navigable for some 25 miles by "doray," and as its waters for the most part are deep and slow flowing, it affords a natural highway to the virgin lands at the back, as well as for sending down the produce.

The land occupied by the British Honduras Fruit Company (formerly Drake's sugar estate) is established in bananas, which appeared to be in a thriving state. The soil is of a deep and free loamy character, exactly suited for this cultivation.

Where the land was virgin forest, newly cleared, the promise of fruit was all that could be desired.

In addition to the two fruit companies mentioned above, several private persons have embarked in the cultivation of bananas, coco-nuts, and cacao on this river, and the prospects are eminently satisfactory. There are large tracts of land about 12 to 15 miles up the river, finer than any below; but during the dry season the communication by river is impeded by shallows and rapids. If this difficulty could be removed, the whole of the Mullin's River valley, stretching to the northern slopes of the Cockscomb Mountains, might be utilised for purposes of cultivation, and an important district opened within easy reach of Belize.

From the mouth of the Mullin's River to the southward, after passing Colston Point, another small settlement has been established at North Stann Creek, where bananas and coco-nuts are being successfully cultivated.

At Commerce Bight, a very promising coco-nut plantation, with some 10,000 trees, between four and six years old, has been established by Mr. C. T. Hunter, which is probably the largest in the colony. In a later chapter I shall deal fully with the nature and characteristics of the different cultivations which came under notice; but I cannot help remarking here, that the whole of the sea-board of British Honduras is eminently fitted for the cultivation of coco-nuts, for which there is always a ready and remunerative market. As the force of the surf is expended on the outer reefs, little sand is accumulated on the coast itself, which, being for the most part low and rich in vegetable humus, affords excellent opportunities for the successful cultivation of coco-nuts.

After passing the mouth of the Sittee River, the next point of interest is All Pines village, in the neighbourhood of which there are two large sugar estates, viz., Regalia and Serpon.

Close to All Pines are the remains of a factory started with the intention of extracting oil from the seeds of the cohune palm (*Attalea cohune*); and not far off are the works of a sawmill, established some years ago with the view of sawing timber from the pitch pine, so abundant in this district. Both were unsuccessful, possibly from want of judgment and capital as much as from the unsuitability of the country at the time for any undertaking requiring skilled manipulation and management.

Regalia sugar estate is under the management of Mr. Reginald Ross, an experienced Demerara planter. It is in excellent order, and furnished with a very complete set of works and buildings. The total area under canes is about 400 acres, the chief variety cultivated being the old Bourbon cane; the produce is shipped almost entirely as ordinary concrete sugar—little or no rum being made.

These latter particulars, I may add, apply to nearly all the sugar estates in British Honduras, of which there are, excluding the Toledo Settlements, altogether at present only about six or seven.

Serpon estate, which adjoins Regalia, is in many respects similarly situated, and is managed by the proprietor, Mr. Bowman.

The labour for sugar estates is supplied by Indians from the neighbouring Republics, by free coolies from Jamaica, or by Jamaica and Belize negroes. The ordinary wages are $7 per month, with rations (pork and flour); or $11 per month without rations. The labourers are hired for twelve months at a time, contracts being strictly regulated by a local labour ordinance, which secures the interest of both master and servant.

The Sittee River, which rises at the foot of the eastern slopes of the Cockscomb Mountains, is navigable probably for some 40 miles of its course; the only barriers to communication being one or two falls (rapids), which, however, are seldom impassable for the long, shallow boats, here called "pit-pans," so much used for river communication.

By the kindness of Mr. Ross we were able to go about 15 miles up the Sittee River, as far as a rapid called Hell Gates. Here the river-bed was so narrowed by rocks that the passage was reduced to about one-third its usual breadth, and being also very steep, a rapid of considerable force was formed.

As the scenery and characteristics of the vegetation along the Sittee River may be accepted as typical of most of the rivers of British Honduras, I will treat of them here a little more fully than I otherwise would. In the first place I may mention that our "pit-pan," a shallow dug out without keel (and with square ends sloping upwards almost like a butcher's tray), was admirably adapted for going up rivers and for passing over shallows and rapids. It was 32 feet long, 2 feet 10 inches wide in the middle, and with low seats placed at equal distances apart. The crew, consisting of four strong Belize creoles, knelt or sat close together in the bow, and paddled with their faces looking up stream. The bowman and the steersman, the latter also a creole, supplied with a paddle, had full control of the "pit-pan," and they generally agreed beforehand what course to take in running falls and rapids, as well as, the particular channel offering the least resistance in going up stream.

Chanting a somewhat monotonous tune, and keeping time with their paddles, the crew in front bend to their work with a will, and soon the "pit-pan" is swiftly sped on its journey. After leaving the settlements, the scenery becomes essentially tropical and luxuriant : passing now between deep, richly-clothed banks and cliffs, which sometimes shut out the strong rays of the sun, we suddenly emerge into open and almost level country, with low, rush-fringed banks, dotted here and there with tall-growing figs and the ubiquitous trumpet-tree. Further inland there would be a "pine ridge," with its clumps of "pitch pine" and "pimento palms," isolated by vast stretches of grassy savannahs.

We would next pass through a densely-wooded forest, consisting of mahogany, cedar, rosewood, &c., with the characteristic vegetation of a "cohune ridge," which extending for a greater or less distance on each side of the river would indicate the richest land of the colony.

On the Sittee River, as on the Mullin's River, the upper portions of their respective valleys have magnificent tracts of "cohune ridge," which are admirably adapted for the successful cultivation of most tropical plants. On our way up the river we landed at a small banana and plantain plantation, opened by Mr. Ross, which, although planted somewhat closely, yielded some of the finest bunches of fruit seen in the colony. Among the bananas there were several young trees of the native rubber-tree (*Castilloa elastica*), thriving well. Cacao here would find an excellent home, and a large plantation might be established with but a small extra expense.

As Mr. Ross has some 48 square miles of land, for the most part adapted for the cultivation of bananas, Liberian coffee, cacao, oranges, nutmegs, mangoes, &c., this instance alone will serve to show what splendid investments await planters in this country, provided they are men of energy and experience, and possess capital sufficient to open up the land in an efficient manner.

The river banks are clothed chiefly with melastomads and caliandras, which form a low fringe of a shrubby character: in most situations the wild cane (*Arundo*) and aquatic grasses exist as dense, tall-growing thickets, close to the water's edge. Here and there are fine handsome trees of wild fig overhanging the river, and in some cases with their huge spreading branches resting almost on the surface of the water. Other trees noticed were, salmwood and quamwood, the latter in abundant flower, and scenting the air for miles round. Numerous trees were completely covered by the rattan cane (*Desmoncus*), which on account of its formidable recurved spines formed an impenetrable barrier to both man and beast.

The higher reaches of the river were bordered by tall, perpendicular banks, composed for the most part of marl and clay: these were afterwards succeeded by bold overhanging cliffs of indurated shale, approaching almost the texture of slate, with here and there a bold conglomerate, or millstone grit. The indurated shale, mentioned above, sometimes occurred in vertical beds, which, running across the river, formed either jutting masses, or rugged, shallow bottoms, giving rise to rapids and falls. When horizontal, these rocks formed huge ledges reaching far out into the river, with caves underneath.

Beyond Hell Gates, the Sittee River has been but little explored. The left branch, rising among the Cockscomb Mountains, passes through a succession of hills and broken country, well timbered with Santa Maria and Yemeri, and being some 2,000 feet to 3,000 feet high, will no doubt in the future afford excellent coffee lands. For the present, at least, there are abundant stretches of rich country below Hell Gates which can be opened and established at a comparatively small cost.

On our return to Regalia, we wished good-bye to our valued friend and host, Mr. Ross, and sailed from All Pines for the south. Stann Creek, just below, has another settlement, lately established for the cultivation of bananas and coco-nuts. The coast all the way down, from All Pines to South Stann Creek, Jonathan Point, False Bay, Placentia Point, and on to Monkey River, is low, and fringed with dense mangrove swamps, with here and there, on banks and ridges, a few villages or settlements with patches of coco-nuts and small cultivations. At Point Jonathan a good coco-nut plantation has been established by Mr. Downer, which is now coming into bearing.

The settlements along the coast, inhabited by Creoles, Caribs, or Spaniards, are generally surrounded by patches of bananas, plantains, and coco-nuts; with cassava, sugar-cane, sweet potato, rice and wanglo, to supply their daily wants.

The settlement at the mouth of the Monkey River may be taken as a typical one for the southern districts, and although composed of the three races mentioned above, viz., Creole, Carib, and Spaniard, living in one settlement, each keeps to its own distinctly marked quarter. The Creoles are generally held to be the most troublesome to control, and they look down upon the Caribs, who for the most part are a quiet, industrious race. The Spaniard-speaking element (of Indian and Spanish blood) is not so numerous in the southern districts as it is north of Belize, and along the western frontier. Its presence here is due, for the most part, to the fact that the proximity of the southern settlements to the Republican States of Guatemala and Spanish Honduras makes them a convenient place of refuge for the lawless and others who render themselves obnoxious or troublesome in their native country. It is interesting to notice that the existence of a Spanish element in a village may often be revealed by the presence of the coco-plum tree (*Chrysobalanus Icaco*), found growing near their dwellings. The fruit is eaten fresh or prepared with sugar, when it forms a favourite conserve with Spaniards all the world over. It is not, I believe, generally known that the kernels of this fruit yield a fixed oil, which might be of service in many instances, where a bland fine oil is desired.

On the Monkey River* the largest fruit company in the colony, viz., the Walize Fruit Company, has opened up an extensive tract of land, and although I was unable to visit it, the accounts given to me would indicate that it is likely to be a great success. The company has a capital of $15,000, in shares of $50 each. Near the mouth of the river, and for some distance

---

* As to the name of this river, Mr. Fowler mentions : "Well may the river be called Monkey River, for all species of the tribe haunt its banks. A drove of baboons surrounded the houses during the night, and the unearthly and dismal choruses, the sepulchral tones and howls of these animals were demoniacal, and would scare any one, hearing them for the first time, in the middle of the night."

up, are large swamps of white mangrove (*Laguncularia racemosa*). The district generally has excellent land for bananas and coco-nuts, but with the exception of those portions bordering the upper reaches of the river, the lands are not continuous, but are distributed in isolated patches or cays, with intervening swamps. Again, higher up the river, the best lands suitable for cultivation are often cut off in the dry season by the shallowness of the river. To obviate this, it is suggested by some, to connect the lands with the coast by a good road; if this were done there is no doubt the Monkey River district would become a very prosperous one. As it is, large quantities of produce are being raised, and the Walize Fruit Company, when in full working, will doubtless establish an important *depôt* here.

Below the mouth of Monkey River is Point Ycacos, on which a small coco-nut plantation has been established by the Hon. Alexander Williamson. There were about 2,500 young plants put out within the last three or four years, and although growing in rather a poor sandy soil they were in good health.

A plantation just being established on a ridge running parallel to the sea was in a very promising situation, being well supplied with vegetable humus and a deep soil. In this young plantation, rice, plantain, and cassava grew well within a few feet of the sea; and no doubt the return from provisions, if systematically worked, would considerably lessen, if not indeed entirely cover, the cost of establishing a coco-nut plantation on this coast.

In the adjoining forest, various species of orchids were gathered, chiefly of *Epidendrum* and *Oncidium*.

A Zamia, probably *Z. prasina*, called locally a "bulrush," was also plentiful on ridges and banks near lagoons. The cabbage palm (*Oreodoxa oleracea*) appears to be utilised in this district for boarding houses, the thatch being obtained from "bay leaf"

(*Sabal*), coco-nut, cohune, or pimento-palm. Often the slender stems of the latter, after being cleaned, are driven into the ground closely together, and they form an excellent stockade, or side walls, for houses. Amongst the Spaniards, it is usual to build the houses with square ends, but the roof is shaped with circular ends overlapping the walls, so as to admit the air freely, but keep out the glare and heat.

Below Point Ycacos, is the mouth of the Deep River, and a large spacious bay, with splendid anchorage, called Port Honduras.

On the banks of the Deep River, and along the shores of Port Honduras, it is said there is the site for a thriving town, if not the capital of the colony. It is easy of access, free from dangerous shoals, and in the immediate neighbourhood of magnificent lands.

Speaking of the district between the Monkey and Deep Rivers, Mr. Fowler remarks: " The formation of the country between these two rivers shows strong indications of minerals, and many specimens of ore have been obtained from the neighbouring hills. Iron, principally with traces of gold and silver, have been found, and a hot sulphur spring bubbles up out of the bed of the Deep River about 30 miles from the mouth."

At the lower, or southern end of Port Honduras, is the landing place for the Seven Hills district. Here is one of the largest sugar estates in the colony, owned by Mr. De Brot, and under the management of Mr. William Morison. The cultivated portions of this estate are very prettily situated, occupying rich sheltered glades and valleys covered by sugar-cane, and surrounded by low rounded wooded hills. The latter are chiefly composed of a finely laminated compact limestone, which yields lime of good quality.

The principal variety of cane cultivated is the Bourbon, which is evidently the favourite in British Honduras, as it is an easy cane to grind and yields well; from its thinner rind and superior sweetness, it is, however, very liable to depredations by rats; but, so far as I could gather, rats have not caused much mischief to canes in this colony.

About 400 acres are under canes at Seven Hills: ratoons are only kept up to the fourth year, it being found more remunerative to plant after that period.

The yield per acre, ranges from $1\frac{3}{4}$ to 2 tons of sugar, the latter being all concrete, with no rum. As this yield is from the natural soil, without manure or special treatment, it speaks well for the quality of land in this district for sugar-cane cultivation. The average rainfall here is a little below 100 inches per annum; the present year (1882) is, however, below the average, and the rainfall is not expected to be above 90 inches.

In riding over the estate with the manager, I noticed that the soil was black on the surface, formed for the most part by the decomposition of the finely laminated limestone; it was very friable on the surface, with a tenacious, unctuous clay beneath; in some instances a quartzy ridge would appear running across the valley, on which the canes did badly; the same remarks apply to a few instances where peroxide of iron cropped up to the surface and gave the soil a fine, shotty, and granular texture. The canes on the whole, however, looked fine and healthy, and the estate generally would compare favourably with that of any other country.

A "fly," or rather a moth, appeared to be troublesome to canes at certain seasons of the year. The different stages of the "fly" are described by Mr. Morison as follows:—"About the end of June or July, a white froth, similar to what is known in England as 'cuckoo spittle,' or 'goat spittle,' appears at the roots of the canes, both under, and above ground. On examination, a small greenish, wingless insect is found embedded in the froth, which remains in this state till about August, when it matures into the 'fly.' While affected in the manner above described, the canes become stunted in growth, but even afterwards, with the mature insect, they are not free from injury, as the 'fly' attacks the leaves and causes them to be spotted and eventually to die off. 'The lower leaves appear to wither first, but the upper leaves are soon attacked, and sometimes so severely, as to cause the whole to fall off, leaving nothing but the bare cane standing. Even among canes not severely attacked, the joints are short and poor. About the end of September and October the 'fly' disappears. The canes after this time, relieved from the attacks of the 'fly,' make very fair growth; the joints become long and full, and they continue to develop, up to cutting time."

To this account Mr. Morison adds that the "fly" is more severe in damp and wet lands in lower portions of the fields than in dry, powdery land.

I obtained specimens of the "fly" for determination, and find it is not at all uncommon on canes in moist districts in other parts of the world. I recommend a dressing of powdered quicklime to the cane stools when the "froth" first appears, and this, together with good drainage, will, I believe, effectually deal with the evil. From this and other districts where cultivation is being carried on, I obtained samples of soil for analysis, and I hope that the local government will be able to place the results of these analyses before planters, in order to indicate the special characteristics of soils in the colony, suitable for different plants.

In the neighbourhood of Seven Hills, beyond the Rio Grande River, is what is termed the Toledo Settlement, established by settlers from Louisiana, in the Southern States of America, after the late war.

The forest between Seven Hills and the Toledo Settlement, is composed of what may be termed a characteristic "cohune ridge." It is a natural forest composed of valuable timber trees such as mahogany, Santa Maria, axe-master, rosewood, augusta, salmwood, sapodilla, &c., with numerous palms. Chief among the latter is the noble cohune palm, which forms about ten per cent. of the forest growth. The ground generally, in the more open parts, was carpeted with selaginellas, ferns, and shade-loving grasses. Under dense shade the undergrowth was very slight, and one could ride almost anywhere under the tall canopy formed by the cohune palms and majestic timber trees.

The Rio Grande River is navigable for dorays some 40 or 50 miles, and it passes through magnificent country, as yet little known. There is no doubt that if this southern district were thoroughly opened, the lands on such rivers as this would soon attract attention and become the seats of thriving industries.

At the Toledo Settlement, which, as mentioned above, is essentially American, about fourteen families settled, a few years ago, in the virgin forest, with little or no capital. But by undaunted courage and perseverance in overcoming the first difficulties, they have succeeded in establishing comfortable homesteads, and in placing under cultivation, chiefly in sugar-cane, some 600 acres of land. The results of the experiment are in many respects most interesting and suggestive. Although in tropical countries, as a rule, the white man is not suited for hard, laborious work in the sun, and it is better for him to possess capital and to employ negroes and coolies for field work, it speaks well for the climate of British Honduras that the white settlers here have, by their own hands, turned a wild tropical forest into a number of apparently rich and prosperous homesteads. Most of the settlers, at present, grow canes and manufacture the produce into common muscovado sugar in open pans. The quality of the sugar made is of a superior kind, most of which is sold locally at prices ranging from $5\frac{1}{2}$ cents to 6 cents per pound.

It is to be hoped, however, that the settlers will, in time, turn attention to other and equally productive industries, such as cacao, nutmegs, oranges, lemons, bananas, coco-nuts, ginger, sarsaparilla, arrowroot, vanilla, black pepper, ground-nuts, and many others, which are admirably adapted for the district, and which can be grown as easily, and with as much certainty of finding a market for them as for sugar.

Cacao has been already tried in one or two instances, and the trees have done well. Cacao-trees, apparently wild, are not uncommonly met with in the forest, so that there is no difficulty here with regard to procuring seeds or plants. Oranges and lemons would thrive in the more stony soils, provided slab rock is not too near the surface. In any case, the top root of such trees as these might very conveniently be removed, when there would be less danger of their coming upon rock. Limes grow apparently wild, and I have no doubt that oranges and lemons would do equally well if once started.

Among the settlers who have established themselves here are Mr. Wilson, at Refuge; the Messrs. Perrot and Mr. Paine, at Mount Hope; Mr. Oetzel; Messrs. Hutchinson and Been, at Mount Royal; Mr. Waterous and son, at Forest House; and Mr. Pearce, at Forest Cottage.

In addition to cultivating sugar, some of the settlers raise cattle, a rich pasture being naturally formed, after the forest is cut down and cleared.

The Toledo Settlement is connected with the sea by a Government road, which is capable of tapping a wide district, and affording an outlet for the despatch of produce, conveniently and expeditiously.

Near the termination of the Government road is Ponta Gorda, a Carib settlement of about 400 inhabitants. This settlement has a resident district magistrate, and is remarkable for its neat and clean appearance. This, no doubt, is somewhat due to the magistrate, Mr. Orgill, who evidently takes care to keep it in a proper sanitary condition.

This is the most southerly settlement in British Honduras, and about 20 miles from the Sarstoon River the boundary between it and the Republic of Guatemala.

Having visited all the settlements in detail, from Belize to Ponta Gorda, we proceeded to retrace our steps to the northward, and having caught the S.S. "City of Dallas" off Mullin's River, reached Belize at noon on the 22nd November.

To the outline of the southern trip given above, I would here add that, thanks to Captain Marriner's local knowledge and careful management, we traversed, with great convenience and success, some 350 miles of the colony, and saw most of its salient features within reach of the settlements.

CHAPTER III.

Trip to western districts. Haul-over. Cramer's Bank. Bridge over Sibun Swamp. John Young's Pine-ridge. Camping out. Butcher Burn's Bank. Limestone Hills. Rich soils. Bush travelling. Gale Creek. Bever Dam. Mahogany forest. Mahogany works. Castile Bank. Prickly bambu. Mount Pleasant. Bad roads. Orange Walk. Government lands for sale. How mahogany is cut. Trucking mahogany. Logwood cutting. Roaring Creek. Savannah Bank. Warree Head Creek. Monkey Fall Savannah. Granny Creek. Mount Hope. The Cayo. Coffee plantation. Position and importance of the Cayo. Communication with Belize. Indian settlement at San Francisco. To Belize by river in doray.

For the tour through the Central and Western Districts, as Captain Marriner's official duties prevented his being able to leave Belize, arrangements were made for me to accompany the Hon. A. Williamson, who had business at Orange Walk, on the Old River. After accomplishing this, he intended to strike across the country through San Pedro, San Jose, Irish Creek, Indian Church, Orange Walk on the New River, and so reach Caledonian Bank and Corosal in the north, where he had arranged to meet a schooner to bring him back to Belize.

As this route offered a good opportunity for seeing the rich valley district of the Old River, as well as the back lands to the west and north, in the neighbourhood of the New River, it was decided that I should accept Mr. Williamson's kind offer to accompany him, and especially as he had the reputation of being an experienced and hardy bush traveller, well acquainted with the country and its people.

Provided with police-horses for riding, and a pack horse to carry our luggage and camping material, we started from Belize about 2 P.M. on the 24th November. The party consisted of Mr. Williamson and myself, Mr. Gillett, a mahogany cutter, my collector, and Mr. Williamson's servant.

We took, in the first instance, the road over the Haul-over, and crossed the town branch of the Old River by a ferry. After passing along the new road through the swamp, we came to Cramer's Bank, used as a cattle pen. To get to the new road leading from Belize to the western frontier, we had to go over a bridge three-quarters of a mile long, which carried the road over the Sibun Swamp.

Owing to the boggy nature of the ground, the pillars of the bridge had sunk in several places, so that the structure presented a somewhat uneven, if not a dangerous surface, especially for the passage of horses. By leading the animals carefully and slowly along we managed, however, to cross the swamp without a mishap. We then found ourselves on John Young's Pine Ridge. It was our intention to cross the pine ridge, and to stop for the night at Butcher Burn's Bank, on the Sibun River.

Owing to rain and darkness overtaking us, we were unable to strike the right track, and eventually had to camp out in the open. But for the rain, sleeping out at night is nothing unusual; but this time we had many disadvantages to contend against, all of which, however, were endured without a murmur, hoping that the next day would find us well on our journey, and sheltered from wind and rain.

Making an early start, we found the rain of the previous night had flooded many portions of the pine ridge, and we did not reach Butcher Burn's Bank until about 11 o'clock.

It is evident that to reach this place the previous day, we should have left Belize early in the morning; but the heavy rain, and the difficulty in crossing the Sibun Swamp, had upset our calculations.

The Sibun River rises on the northern slopes of the Cockscombs, far to the south. Its mouth is near Wagner village, some 10 miles below Belize. In the interior, it passes through a considerable extent of hilly country, with limestone rocks, forming sharply-pointed peaks and ridges, giving a picturesque character to the scenery. At the foot of these hills the soil is remarkably deep and rich, and with a good water-way for produce, and its proximity to Belize, this district will no doubt soon attract attention.

After leaving Butcher Burn's Bank, we once more struck across John Young's Pine Ridge, this time going due north and making for Gale Creek, a tributary of the Old River.

After travelling for some hours, during which I managed to gather numerous orchids and seeds, we entered an old and very much overgrown track in a cohune ridge, which was intended to take us to Beaver Dam. After crossing with considerable difficulty one or two swampy creeks, and cutting our way through tangled masses of "tie-ties" and fallen trees, rain and darkness once more overtook us, and we camped for the night on the banks of Gale Creek. With some difficulty, owing to the damp character of the brushwood, we managed to make a fire to cook our supper, and although the place was swarming with mosquitoes, and heavy showers fell during the night, we managed to get a little rest.

We were early on foot the next morning, to make arrangements for a long stage to Castile Bank and Orange Walk. The cohune ridge through which we passed was full of numerous orchids and aroids hanging in festoons from the trees. As most of the mahogany had been cut some years ago, the trees left were small and undersized, but the indications of the soil were all that could be desired for most cultivations of a tropical character.

The best mahogany is said to be found to the north of the river Belize. In consequence of the nature of the soil in that district, in which there is a great quantity of limestone, the mahogany is longer in coming to maturity: but when full grown, it is of a harder and firmer texture than that which is found in the southern portion of the settlement.

After following the disused track for some miles, we eventually came out on the Old River at a spot called Beaver Dam. It may be mentioned here that numerous places in the colony marked and named on maps are at present in existence only as names. At one time or other they were mahogany works or temporary depôts (banks), where workmen's huts were built, and where logs were trimmed preparatory to being tumbled into the river, and floated down the stream. When the mahogany in the district was exhausted the works were abandoned, the huts in course of time tumbled to pieces, and the place eventually would become so overgrown as to be hardly distinguishable from the neighbouring forest. The name, however, lives in the memories of the inhabitants, and is handed down until it becomes a mere tradition. Such a place was Beaver Dam. There was no vestige of a dwelling: in fact, nothing but tall, rank-growing weeds, overtopping our horses. We pushed on parallel to the river course, keeping on its right bank until we came to Castile Bank. Our course was chiefly over old mahogany tracks, where logs had been "trucked" or "slided" during the previous season. Owing to the heavy rains of the previous week, the track, already well worked by cattle, was simply a " bog route," and at every step the horses sank up to their knees in black, tenacious mud.

At Castile Bank we found a small mahogany and cedar works

in working order, with numerous logs in course of being trimmed, or "manufactured," preparatory to being tumbled into the river. After a slight halt for breakfast, and for drying our clothes, we pushed on, keeping still on the right bank of the river. Soon after, we passed through some magnificent cohune forests, interspersed near the river's bank with the thick matted growth of the "prickly bambu." This plant is one of the most graceful and handsome of the family; its leaves being as fine as asparagus, and its long sinuous stems drooping in a most graceful manner. Seen at a distance, a vast expanse of this bambu gives one the idea of a downy, feathery mass of green, most attractive and refreshing. Here, however, its beauty and elegance ends. On nearer acquaintance it develops into one of the most formidable obstacles which a traveller can meet. Every joint of its long slender stem is furnished with a formidable *coterie* of spines, sometimes an inch or an inch and a half long.

Where this bambu has firmly established itself—as along the river banks—it is quite impossible to pass through it; even wild animals avoid it, or if hotly pressed, and they take shelter there, they are literally torn to pieces by its ruthless spines.

Our path often led over creeks running into the Old River, and, where particularly dangerous, we had to dismount and lead our horses across; at other times we had to allow them to take their own lead and get over ourselves the best way we could.

The vegetation along the banks of the Old River was of surpassing beauty and luxuriance. As the chief objects of the woodcutter are the mahogany, cedar, and rosewood, everything else is left alone. Magnificent trees of the *Ceiba*, or silkcotton-tree, were passed, with buttresses like those of huge castles. The first branches were generally some 80 or 100 feet from the ground. Above, their wide-spreading massive branches were literally clothed with orchids, wild pines, and a perfect garden of parasitic vegetation. Hanging along the stems were numerous "lianes," or "withes," here called "tie-ties," looking like the festooned ropes of a ship.

Here and there we passed a space near the river bank a little more open than others, where mahogany works had once stood, but now lapsing fast into the original jungle. It is said that a mahogany forest can be cut every thirty years; hence many of these abandoned mahogany works are re-opened after a longer or shorter interval, and become, for a time, at least, once more the scenes of daily toil, and the busy abode of man. Now, however, they were silent and deserted, the mid-day calm being only broken by the titter of bright-plumaged birds, or the solitary cry of some wild animal.

In the course of the afternoon we passed Mount Pleasant, another mahogany bank, in working order, and after crossing a beautifully clear stream, falling over rocks encrusted with limestone deposits, and beautifully margined with elegant ferns, we entered the forest in the neighbourhood of Orange Walk, the object of Mr. Williamson's journey.

Here we met numerous mahogany tracks, all converging on the settlement, and just about dusk we left the forest and entered the savannah, or pasture surrounding the settlement, dotted here and there with the huts of the workpeople; among these, in an open space, stood Mr. Gillett's house, where we were hospitably entertained for the night.

Owing to the bad condition of the roads after the late heavy rains, and the unfavourable accounts we received of the creeks and tracks in the neighbourhood of San Pedro, San Jose, Irish Creek, and Indian Church, it was thought impossible to carry out our intended trip to the north, and much to my regret we had to abandon it. Under these circumstances, Mr. Williamson decided to return to Belize by boat, and get to Caledonian Bank and Corosal by sea; while I elected to remain up-country, and explore the upper portions of the valley of the Old River, and, if possible, push on to the Cayo, or western frontier station.

After one day's rest at Orange Walk, during which the plants collected on the journey from Belize were examined and dried, and after taking a short section through the forest for the purpose of seeing the country towards the left branch of the Sibun River to the south, I left Orange Walk with a guide, for the western frontier.

The valley of the Old River through which we passed gradually widened as we travelled to the westward, and numerous mahogany works (banks) were dotted on each side of the river, each having so many miles of frontage, and reaching far into the backwoods. It appears that the land tax on mahogany and logwood works is estimated at $8 per mile base. Having seen one mahogany works, with the exception of the difference in the scenery, and varying circumstances of soil and climate, the details are much the same.

Most of the mahogany forests are in the hands of a few proprietors, who, to preserve their young trees, as a rule, discourage settling. They adopt a rude system of forest conservancy, backed by a very strict trespass law, which entirely prevents the land from being alienated or used as provision grounds by settlers. This feeling, in a measure, is, no doubt, the outcome of the old terms on which the English were permitted to hold the settlement, viz., that they were debarred from making plantations, or in any way making permanent homes in the colony.

Government land may be bought at a dollar an acre, or, if preferred, short leases of five years are issued to persons desirous to occupy waste lands of the Crown, not less than fifty acres, at a yearly rent of 10 cents an acre, with right to purchase at any time during the tenancy.

When it is intended to open a mahogany works on any part of an estate, the first step is to employ a "hunter," or experienced woodman, who spends several days alone prospecting in the forest. After an absence, longer or shorter according to circumstances, during which he often suffers many privations, the hunter returns and reports the number and character of suitable mahogany-trees to be found within easy reach of the works, the latter being always placed at a convenient spot on the bank of the river, where the mahogany logs can be manufactured and easily tumbled into the river.

The "hunter" is paid so much for every tree which, on examination, is found suitable for cutting, *i.e.*, squaring 18 inches and upwards. The next step is to open a track to it and proceed to cut it down. Owing to the huge buttresses which many mahogany-trees possess, a platform is sometimes erected so as to enable the men to cut the tree above them. When lopped, cleaned, and sawn to the available length, the log is ready to be hauled to the works.

During the dry months of the year the logs are carried on trucks drawn by bullocks. The truck is a ponderous framework, mounted on four broad wheels about 3 feet in diameter, with 9 inches tread, the latter being made in a most primitive fashion by sawing pieces across from a log of Santa Maria. During wet weather, when the ground is too soft for the trucks to travel, mahogany is drawn on slides, or a kind of sleigh, which passes over "skids." The latter consist of long, hard wood posts, about 3 inches in diameter, placed across the track about a yard apart.

Being imbedded in mud, the fresh slippery bark affords a suitable and handy surface for the passage of the slide with its heavy load. Sometimes mahogany logs are drawn, in the manner above described, distances of 8 or 10 miles.

Mahogany is always trucked in the middle of the night, the cattle not being able to perform such laborious work during the heat of the day. It is a picturesque and striking scene, this midnight trucking.

"The lowing of the oxen, the creaking of the wheels, the shrill cries of the men, the resounding cracks of their whips, and the red glare of the pine torches in the midst of the dense, dark forest, produce an effect approaching to sublimity."

At the works the logs are regularly squared and prepared for the market.

If, however, they are likely to be chafed and injured in transit, by going down shallow creeks, the squaring is done at Belize, or at the river's mouth.

Trucking is generally carried on during the months of April and May, when the ground is hard after a long period of dry weather. About the middle of June, after the May "seasons," or rains, the rivers are swollen, and advantage is taken of this opportunity to tumble the logs into the water, and float them down to about 10 miles from the river's mouth. Here a large iron chain, or "boom," is fixed, which stops the logs as they float down. At this point the several owners select the logs by their respective marks, form them into rafts, and so float them down to the sea, and ultimately to Belize, whence they are shipped abroad.

Logwood cutting appears to be a much simpler and much less laborious work. After the trees, which are seldom more than a foot in diameter, but often only half this size, are cut down, the outer or sap wood is removed, leaving nothing but the inner dark-coloured heart wood. When thus prepared, the logwood is carried on trucks or "crooked" to the nearest bank, where, to prevent it from sinking, it is packed in "bark logs," or light, buoyant cradles, capable of carrying a ton or two of logwood. An immense train of these heavily-freighted "bark logs" is often met with on its way down the river, or anchored at night in the middle of the stream.

Most of the logwood is found in damp, moist districts to the north; but there are also many tracts to the south, where logwood is very plentiful.

After passing Roaring Creek and Savannah Bank, we came to Tea Kettle, where we joined once more the main road from Belize to the western frontier. In many places, the road is so overgrown with bush and obstructed by fallen trees, as to be scarcely recognisable.

At length we came to a stony and somewhat hilly country near Warree Head Creek, with a good view of extensive country covered by a rich tropical forest.

Monkey Fall Savannah appears to offer a good site for a fine cattle pen, with a plentiful supply of good water.

After crossing Granny Creek we reached Mount Hope, an old settlement in an advanced state of decay, and with but few huts remaining.

After some ten hours in the saddle, and numerous divergencies from the regular track, to examine and explore the forest, I was glad to accept a night's rest from Mr. Gillett, uncle of my host at Orange Walk, who kindly offered every comfort which his small house could afford.

Early next morning, leaving my collector at Mount Hope, I pushed on for the Cayo, crossing Little Barton Creek and Great Barton Creek, both greatly swollen after heavy rains.

The road next went through Tiger Run, a large mahogany works, in a magnificent district. The forest here had fine indiarubber-trees and pimento, the latter being a tall tree, finer than any I had ever seen before.

The woods also were fragrant with the ripe bursting pods of vanilla, which hung in festoons from the trunks of Santa Maria and other rough-barked trees.

The Cayo was reached about noon, and I called upon Mr. Travers, the newly-appointed magistrate of this remote frontier station.

One of the chief inducements which drew me to the Cayo was to see a coffee estate about two miles beyond, under charge of M. Vivenot. In company with the latter, whom I fortunately met at the Cayo, and Mr. Blanconeaux, we proceeded up the western branch of the Belize River, until we came to a deep, rich, well-sheltered valley surrounded by low wooded hills.

Here about 100 acres had been cleared and established in coffee under the shade of bananas, with corn as an intermediary crop. The coffee-trees, about 30,000, were from one to two years old, planted out. Seed had been obtained from Martinique, Trinidad, and Guatemala. As a whole, the plantation was in a promising state; in some cases the trees were overshaded by bananas, and consequently the plants were weak and "spindled." There is no doubt, also, that the ground had been somewhat impoverished by the large crop of corn (maize) which was then being taken off.

Most of the trees about two years old were, however, bearing their first crop, and looked as if, even at this early age, some two or three hundredweights per acre would be yielded by them. The plantation was well laid out, with roads and intervals of 18 feet dividing the blocks. Naturally, being a pioneering effort, the best mode of procedure adapted to the district could not be obtained at once; and, again, the difficulty of obtaining labour had hampered the undertaking and increased the expenses.

I left the plantation, however, with a favourable impression respecting the possibility of growing good coffee in British Honduras, and I have no doubt that if Coolie labour could be obtained, the whole of this western district would soon be dotted over with prosperous plantations. The cost of clearing and cleaning land ready for planting is put down at £6 per acre; the labourers, at present, owing to the remoteness of the district, get from 42 to 50 cents per day.

I returned to the Cayo, or the Cay, which, from its position nearly on the frontier line between British territory and that of the Republic of Guatemala, possesses more importance than its appearance and size would indicate.

It is connected with Belize by the Government road already mentioned, and this leads over the frontier to Peten and other towns in Guatemala. A fair amount of trade is carried on between Belize and Peten by way of the Cayo; merchandise being either carried all the way by mules, or partly by river.

This little frontier station occupies a picturesque position at the junction of the two branches of the Belize River. The principal houses are those of the magistrate, the court-house, and the headquarters of the police, situated on the higher ground; while below, and extending to the point where the two rivers meet, is an open savannah, affording pasturage for cattle, and dotted here and there with the thatched huts of the natives.

The entire population is about 300.

With the appointment of Mr. Travers, a highly-educated and accomplished officer, as magistrate, the Cayo is destined to increase in importance and character, and as it is proposed to organise a regular system of water communication by a Government "pit-pan" with Belize, the settlement will be brought into closer connection with the headquarters of the Government.

In returning from the Cayo I experienced very wet and

uncomfortable weather, with swollen creeks and mahogany tracks, if possible, more muddy and disagreeable than before.

My guide having disappointed me, I was fortunate to meet with a brave little boy called "Doctor," a protégé of Mr. Williamson's, who safely piloted me a distance of some 15 miles through rain and darkness, until we reached Mount Hope about 11 o'clock at night.

At Tea Kettle I met Mr. Gillett, of Orange Walk, who took me through the Indian settlement of San Francisco, and eventually to Orange Walk.

From Orange Walk I determined to return to Belize by the Old River, and making an early start on Friday morning we reached Belize about 8 o'clock the following evening.

The numerous botanical and other notes made on this journey will more fittingly come under a description of the plants and general resources of the colony, and I will therefore defer them to a later chapter.

CHAPTER IV.

Flora of British Honduras. First impressions of the country. Mangrove-trees. Characteristics of vegetation of the interior dependent on geological features. Underlying strata. How deposited. Geological floor. Glacial action. Icebergs. Reasons for adopting glacial theory. Pine-ridge country. Vegetation. Pine-trees, pimento-thatch, crabboe, haha. Distribution of pine-ridges. Use of pine-wood. White and yellow pine. Resin and turpentine from pine-trees. How to extract turpentine. Cohune-ridge. Cohune-palm. Description: leaves, stem, and fruit. Cohune seeds. Oil. Timber-trees. Mahogany. Value of export. Common cedar. Logwood. Sapodilla. Santa Maria. Fiddle-wood. Rosewood. Salmwood. Braziletto. Ironwood. Mahoe. Numerous undetermined woods. Locust-tree. Cashaw. Edible candle-tree. Palms. Orchids. Ferns.

THE flora of British Honduras, from its relations, on the one hand, to the Continental forms of Central America, as well as to those of the neighbouring West Indian Archipelago, might naturally be expected to exhibit many types common to these districts, in addition to not a few peculiar to it, on account of the exceptional conditions of soil and climate which obtain therein. The first impressions of a visitor to British Honduras are associated with the almost continuous growth of mangrove-trees, which, covering the numerous "cays," or small islands out in the offing, have also taken entire possession of the low coast-line on the mainland, tending to give the country, from the outside, a densely wooded appearance. These extensive forests of mangrove in themselves are useful for no purpose whatever, if we except the fact that the bark of some species is used for tanning purposes. Where, however, through the agency of the mangrove-trees, soil has accumulated, and land has been formed, patches or "banks" of this character form splendid localities for coco-nut plantations, and they are being utilised in this manner, both on the cays, as well as along the coast-line.

In the interior, the vegetation is greatly diversified; but as the changes in its character appear to be so closely associated with the geological features of the country, a few remarks on the main elements of these features may not be uninteresting.

As may be gathered from a preceding chapter, British Honduras occupies a strip of country, running due north and south, parallel to the sea, and with the high central range, or dividing mountain zone of Central America, immediately at its back. In general, the land rises from the sea coast, in a gentle slope towards the west. Numerous rivers take their rise in the central chain, and these, flowing to the eastward, form deep, slow-flowing rivers, suitable for navigation, and forming natural water-ways to the interior. The underlying strata, composed of quartzy rocks, with here and there carbonaceous shales, sandstone rocks, and limestone, crop up in the low, detached ranges which intersect the country to the west and south of Belize, as well as in the steep, rugged elevations of the Cockscomb country to the south. Judging by the nature of the rocks, and *detritus* brought down by the rivers, the central chain of mountains, forming the western frontier of the colony, is composed chiefly of quartzy and felspathic rocks and sandstones of great age, which have been upheaved into their present position under circumstances similar to those which have formed their vast extensions, the Rocky Mountains to the north, and the Andean system to the south. The geological floor of British Honduras, if I may use the term, appears to have been formed by the disintegration and removal of the rocks from the central chain in the west, and their distribution by the action of water or ice over the lowlands to the east. It is maintained by some, that large glaciers covered certain portions of Central America during the glacial period, and the conditions induced by these are said to account for the presence of boulder-clay in valleys and certain hog-backed hills, as well as the transportation of large scratched boulders, noticed in some of the countries on either side of the central chain.* Mr. Belt states that the presence of glaciers in Central America would afford a solution of many phenomena that otherwise would be inexplicable. After mentioning the main points in favour of the existence of glaciers, he adds that the scarcity of alluvial gold in the valley of Santa Domingo, and other places in Nicaragua, points in the same direction. Glacier ice scoops out all the contents of the valleys, and in deepening them does nor sort the materials like running water, or the action of the waves upon the sea coast. As regards gold-bearing quartz, when the denuding agent was water, the rocks were worn away and the heavier gold was left behind, at the bottom of the alluvial deposits; but when the denuding agent was glacier ice, the stony masses and their metallic contents were carried away or mingled together in the unassorted moraines. The evidence of glacial action, if they exist at all in British Honduras, must be looked for in the higher mountain valleys in the west, and possibly in those of the Cockscomb Mountains, or their spurs to the south. If, as was supposed, ice covered the higher ranges and descended in great glaciers only as low as the line of country now standing at two thousand feet above the sea, then very little of the actual surface of British Honduras would have been subject to direct glacial action. It is, however, quite possible that the transportation of rocks from the central chain and their distribution over the sea bottom so as to form the foundations of the country, may have been accomplished by floating icebergs.

---

* "The Naturalist in Nicaragua," pp. 259-274.

Later, as the land gradually emerged from the sea, water would accumulate in the hollows, river systems would be formed, and the finer *débris* brought down from the interior would be continuously deposited, forming soils suitable for the growth of plants.

Where the original quartzy rocks, in the form of a bold conglomerate, gravel or fine sand derived from the central zone, appear on the surface, they give rise to extensive tracts of undulating, or comparatively level country, known locally as "pine-ridges," so called from the prevalence upon them of trees of the yellow pine (*Pinus cubensis*).

These tracts, as may be expected, possess a shallow, poor soil; and they are covered only by hardy, coarse grasses, of little value for pasturing purposes except in a young succulent state. The pines mentioned above are dotted over the country in small clumps or singly, giving it an open, park-like appearance. Associated with the clumps of pine-trees is a small, slender, fan-leaved palm, known locally as "pimento thatch": the stem of this palm, after being cleaned of its investing coat of fibre, is used for fences, sides of houses, and generally, where a tough, slender pole is required. Another common "pine-ridge" plant in the south is the "crabboe," which yields a kind of plum or cherry, sometimes used for food, and whose bark is used for tanning; as, also, the "haha," a wild fig, whose leaves are so rough that they are an excellent substitute for sandpaper. To the west, in the neighbourhood of Roaring Creek, the ordinary pine-ridge plants give place to groves of oak (probably *Quercus virens*). Some of these oaks attain great size, often measuring 50 feet to the first branches, and correspondingly large in girth. The pine-ridges of the colony occupy slightly rising country, generally at some distance inland from the rivers and the coast. In the north there is a large pine-ridge running north, between the Hondu and the New Rivers, almost all the way from Indian Church to Corosal. Another large pine-ridge exists to the west of Alligator Pond, and between it and the mouth of the Northern River.

To the north of the Belize River, an extensive pine-ridge occupies the country between it and New River lagoon, some 20 or 25 miles across. To the south of the river Belize, there is John Young's pine-ridge, over which passes the road to the western frontier, and which should also greatly facilitate the construction of a railway in the same direction.

In the neighbourhood of All Pines, as already noticed, there is a large pine-ridge connected by several other smaller ones, so that a person might ride continuously over an open, park-like country, for some thirty or forty miles. It is estimated that about one-third of the area of British Honduras, at present known, is composed of pine-ridge country, having the geological and botanical characteristics above indicated.

The pine (*Pinus cubensis*), the chief plant of the pine-ridges, is probably the most abundant tree in the colony; but the timber is used locally to a small extent only for building purposes, owing, it is said, to the difficulty experienced in sawing it. The wood is heavy, and, if properly seasoned, might be very durable. Its chief use at present, however, is as fuel, and in making torches. The latter are extensively used at the mahogany works; and, indeed, but for the pine torches the hauling of mahogany, which, on account of the heat and the flies (mosquitoes), takes place chiefly at night, could not be carried on. For railway sleepers, the pine-wood, carefully selected, should prove most valuable. There is an impression in the colony that two species of pine exist on the pine-ridges, which are distinguished as white and yellow pine, and supposed to be characterised in the one case by rather smooth and compact bark, and in the other by rather thick, spongy, and rough bark. I was, however, unable to distinguish any difference in the trees pointed out to me as a white and a yellow pine, the botanical characters of both being exactly the same. In addition to the utilisation of the timber, as mentioned above, and especially by the aid of efficient steam saw-mills, other products might be obtained from them. For instance, if properly tapped, resin of good quality, and in large quantities, should be available; and the wood, by distillation, might yield both turpentine and tar. In the Southern States of America turpentine is obtained from a nearly allied tree, viz., the pitch, or yellow pine (*Pinus australis*), as follows:—" Cavities or boxes are made in the trunks of the trees as they stand. They are made from 6 to 12 inches above the ground, and are mostly cut deep enough into the wood to hold about a quart. From one to four boxes are made in each trunk. The wood is hacked away above the box, or channels are made leading to it, down which the turpentine flows. When the box is full it is removed by a spoon or ladle, and placed in barrels. The first year's flow of turpentine thus obtained is known as Virgin dip, or Virgin turpentine. Some of this crude turpentine is exported, but it is mostly distilled in the neighbourhood of the turpentine orchards. Oil of turpentine, or, as it is often called, spirit of turpentine, is distilled from the oleo-resin as collected, either with or without water. It is used in enormous quantities in the preparation of varnishes, paints, and for various other purposes in the arts and manufactures, as well as in medicine."

Next to the pine-ridge lands, the most strongly-marked feature in the surface of British Honduras are the "cohune-ridges," which, as they contain chiefly the rich valuable soils of the colony, deserve special notice. The term "cohune-ridge" (Spanish corosal) is applied to the low-lying lands generally bordering river valleys, or occupying extensive tracts or basins, as in the west and south, or at the heads of some of the river-systems. Geologically speaking, a "cohune-ridge" has been formed by a river valley, or depression in the quartzy ground-floor of the country, being, in process of time, filled up by large deposits of fine alluvium and vegetable *débris* brought down from the interior by means of rivers. Hence a cohune-ridge soil is deep, rich, and very abundantly supplied with nitrogenous compounds, affording splendid food for plants.

As its name indicates, a cohune-ridge has, as its characteristic plant, the noble cohune-palm (*Attalea cohune*), which is one of the noblest members of the palm family. In a cohune-ridge this palm, in different stages of its growth, forms probably 20, and in some cases 30, per cent. of the vegetation, the remainder being composed either of mahogany, cedar, rosewood, sapodilla, Santa Maria, the smaller palms, or shade-loving trees. The cohune-palm, especially before it has formed a stem, has a magnificent spread with its large pinnate leaves, sometimes covering an area fully a hundred feet in diameter. In the neighbourhood of Tiger Run, near the public road, where there was an open sheltered spot, a frond of this palm was estimated to be 60 feet long and 8 feet in breadth. After the stem is formed the fronds become much smaller, and when the palm has attained a height, as many do, of 50 or 60 feet, the fronds are apparently not larger than those of the oil palm (*Elæis guineensis*).

The cohune bears a nut growing in large bunches, and produced annually, some $2\frac{1}{2}$ feet long, hanging down from near the bases of the leaves like huge clusters of grapes—reminding one of the old sacred representations of the ponderous clusters from the Promised Land carried by the Hebrew spies. Each nut is of the size and shape of a pheasant's egg, covered on the outside by a thin layer of fibrous husk, and composed internally of a hard shell with three cells, containing as many horny oily seeds. These seeds yield a valuable oil, which is used locally for burning, and feeding pigs, the husk being given to fowls.

The country people extract oil from the cohune-nuts in the following manner. When the nuts are what they term full, they break between two stones the shell, which is very hard; they then pound the kernel for some time in a wooden mortar, and the mass is put intô a boiler with water, and boiled down until all the oil, or fat, floats. They skim the oil off, fry it in an iron pot, so as to disengage all the aqueous particles, and then bottle it. By this simple process the average yield is one quart bottle of oil from one hundred nuts. When in full bearing a cohune-palm bears one or two, and sometimes three, bunches of fruit, with an average of five hundred nuts to the bunch.

Several attempts have been made to establish an industry in connection with the extraction of oil from the cohune-nuts, but so far without success. The chief difficulties appear to be connected with breaking the hard, dense shell surrounding the kernels, and the small proportion which exists between the latter and the general mass of the nut. When properly prepared, however, the oil is said to be superior to that of the coco-nut, and to burn twice as long—that is, a pint of the former is said to burn as long as a quart of the latter. Considering that cohune oil is marketable in England "in any quantity at the price of the finest and purest coco-nut oil," it is a matter of regret that the scores of tons of cohune-nuts found wild in the woods of British Honduras do not contribute anything to the wealth of the colony.

Returning, however, to the characteristic vegetation of a cohune-ridge, after the cohune-palm the most striking objects in the forest are the majestic timber-trees, whose huge stems reach far out of sight, and are lost in the dense canopy of vegetation above. Chief amongst the timber-trees of the colony comes the mahogany (*Swietenia mahogani*), which, with logwood, forms the staple article of export. The average quantity of mahogany shipped from British Honduras during the last five years amounts to nearly 3,000,000 feet, of the annual value of £30,000.

The best qualities of mahogany, as already mentioned, come from the limestone soils to the north of Belize: those from the south, and especially from the Mosquito Coast, being deficient in density and fine grain, are known in England as baywood, hence "baymen," a term often applied to the mahogany-cutters of these coasts. Although the mahogany near the coast and within easy reach of the principal rivers has been for the most part cut down and shipped, there is a considerable quantity of mahogany left in the country and still available, especially by means of railways, to supply the European and American markets for many years to come.

Growing with the mahogany is a member of the same family, the common cedar (*Cedrela odorata*), which is in great demand for light indoor work, and from which the fragrant boxes for Havannah cigars are made. In the colony the trunks of the largest trees are hollowed out to make bungays, dorays, pitpans, and canoes, purposes for which, on account of the light and durable character of the wood, they are admirably adapted. The export of British Honduras cedar for the last five years amounts, on an average, to about 130,000 feet. Logwood, which really comes next to mahogany in export value, is found in rather moist lands to the north and west, where it forms immense thickets; but it is not characteristic of what is termed strictly cohune land. The logwood-trees—about 15 or 20 feet high—have some points of resemblance in appearance and habit of growth to trees of the white thorn in England. The stems and young branches, at first grey, become afterwards of a dark colour; the trunks are perpendicularly ribbed, or columnar, and when cut down the outer white, or sapwood, is removed, leaving only the reddish or dark heart-wood, which is split into convenient logs suitable for shipment. It is claimed for Honduras logwood that it is superior to that grown in Jamaica and St. Domingo, and that its market value is fully 40 per cent. higher. Amongst other forest trees of British Honduras are the sapodilla (*Sapota achras*), a very handsome wood, but so heavy that it cannot be floated down the rivers; the Santa Maria (*Calophyllum calaba*), very suitable for shingles and heavy machine work and buildings, its seeds also yield an abundant oil suitable for lamps; fiddle-wood (*Citharexylum sp.*); rose-wood (*Dalbergia sp.*), a dark, rich, reddish wood with fine grain, greatly in request for cabinet purposes, but, like the sapodilla, so heavy that it cannot be floated down the rivers, and hence very difficult to get out in fine large logs; salmwood (*Jacaranda sp.*); dogwood (*Piscidia erythrina*); braziletto (*Cæsalpinia brasiliensis*); ironwood (*Laplacea hæmatoxylan*); and the pix, or bastard Lignum vitæ.

The mahoe (*Paritium elatum*) yields a darkish-green wood of great value; as also the celebrated Cuba bast, an article of commerce prepared from the inner layers of the bark. I obtained numerous other specimens of very fine-grained and beautifully-marked woods, unknown to commerce, but very abundant in the backwoods of the colony. The following are some of the local names of woods, which remain to be determined when good botanical specimens can be obtained. They are: axemaster, ironwood, cabbage-bark, pigeon-wood, turtle-bone, augusta, candle-wood, redwood, palmalata, poison-wood, polewood, wynaka, bull-hoof, billy-web, grape, mountain-plum, nasex, and half-crown. The ziricote is a beautiful wood, somewhat scarce, which has been exported from time to time in small quantities. It has much of the appearance in its bold markings to the celebrated calamander wood of Ceylon, and I doubt not it would make furniture of great beauty and value.

Along the banks of rivers one of the commonest objects is the locust-tree (*Hymenæa courbaril*), said to yield a tough, close-grained timber. A resin resembling gum-anime exudes from the trunk, and is found in lumps at the bases of old trees. The cashaw (*Prosopis juliflora*) also yields a hard durable wood, as well as a gum resembling gum-arabic. The pods in Jamaica are used as food for cattle, but they are likely to be very injurious if eaten when partially germinated, that is, after rains.

In the Savannah, near Orange Walk (Old River), there are two or three fine trees of the edible candle-tree (*Parmentiera edulis*). The fruit, like long-ribbed, soft calabashes, is eaten in some parts of Central America, under the name of Quauhxilotl, or Cuajilote.; but the chief use of the plant is evidently to supply food for cattle, horses, and pigs, which greedily devour the fruit as soon as it falls. Other trees supplying food for cattle, &c., are the ramoon (*Trophis americana*) and the bread-nut (*Brosimum alicastrum*), both of which keep horses, especially, in excellent condition.

In addition to pine-ridge and cohune-ridge, there is sometimes known a district possessing a vegetation of its own, to which the colonists apply the term "broken-ridge." This broken-ridge country generally appears to lie on the outside, and generally parallel to and continuous with the cohune-ridge; and, in fact, is an intermediate belt of vegetation coming between it and the pine-ridge country. The trees in this belt are smaller than in the cohune-ridge; the undergrowth is denser and more scrubby in character; and, generally, the conditions indicate a poorer and less luxuriant phase of plant

F 2

life, toning down more and more until it merges into the scant, sparse vegetation of the pine-ridge country. Often, the belt of intermediary low growth between the coast and the virgin forests is termed broken-ridge; but, in this case, it is one that has probably been artificially formed by abandoned cultivated areas, and does not occur under the conditions which obtain in the natural state. The broken-ridge is no doubt due to a difference in the character of the soil, which, having a slight depth only of humus and alluvium, is able to support a less luxuriant vegetation than the cohune-ridge,* but a little more so than the pine-ridge, which is almost devoid of these important elements of plant food.

Starting from a river-bed, and traversing the country at right angles to its course, there first comes the cohune country, then the broken-ridge, and lastly the pine-ridge. The latter generally acts as a watershed between the several river basins, and the order in which the ridges come may be shown as follows :—

| Cohune ridge | River | Cohune ridge | — | Broken ridge | — Pine-ridge — | Broken ridge | — | Cohune ridge | River |

The vegetation of the cohune-ridge comprises tall-towering timber-trees, the lordly mahogany and luxuriant palms; while the ground below is covered with shade-loving ferns, selaginellas, and aroids. The broken-ridge has fewer, less luxuriant, and somewhat stunted timber-trees, such as the cockspur, abundant in prickles and thorns; the supa, or gru-gru palm (*Acrocomia sclerocarpa*), and small-leaved spiny shrubs of *Randia, Capparis*, &c. In the more open spaces, coarse bromeliads, rank

---

* The term "ridge" is not quite applicable, as often a cohune-ridge, for instance, is really a valley. It is more applicable in the case of pine-ridge, where probably the term had its origin, but the terms are here used as understood in the country.

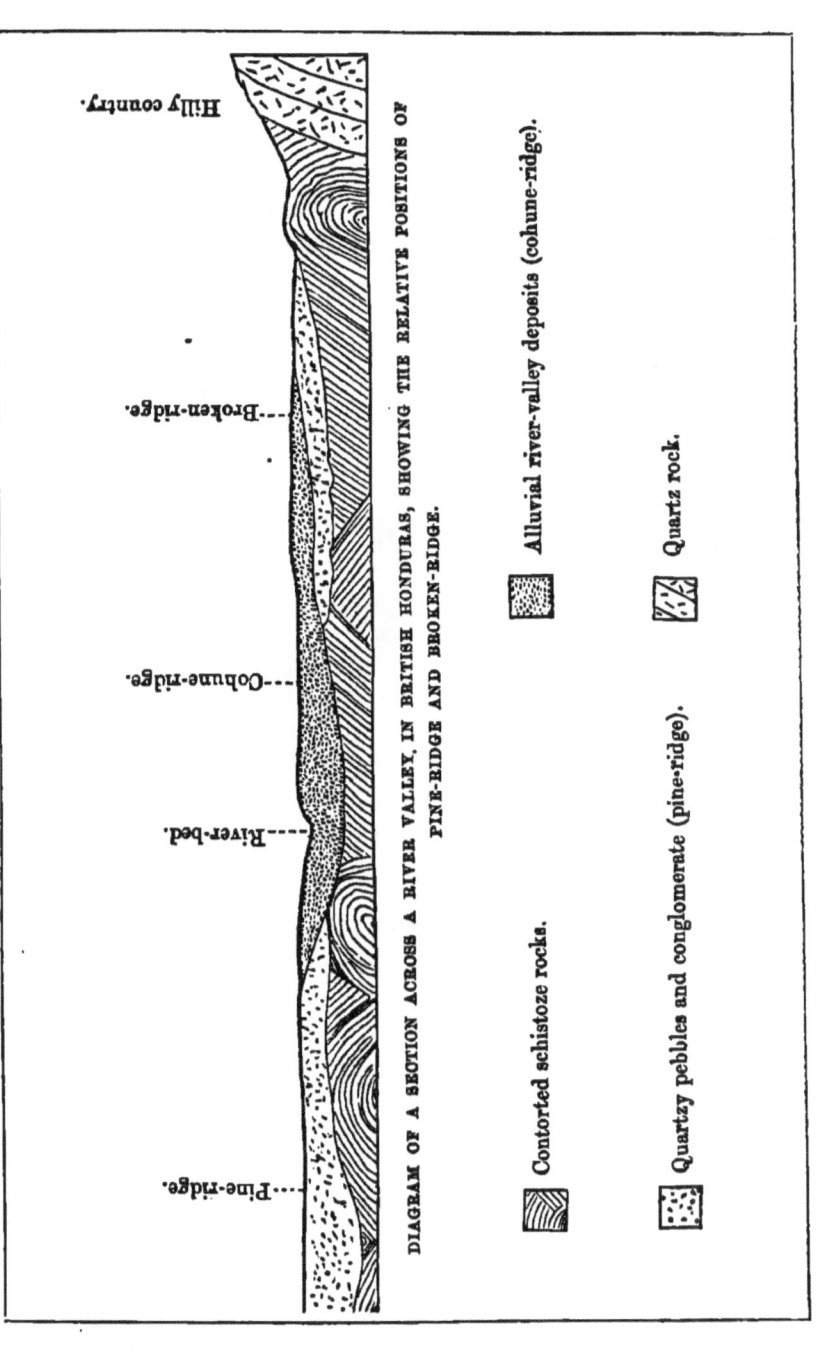

DIAGRAM OF A SECTION ACROSS A RIVER VALLEY, IN BRITISH HONDURAS, SHOWING THE RELATIVE POSITIONS OF PINE-RIDGE AND BROKEN-RIDGE.

grasses, and prickly creepers impede one's movements until, at last, the open pine-ridge country is reached. Here, as already mentioned, the tall (Scotch-looking) firs, or pines, are the more striking objects, surrounded, when in clumps, by the shrubby pimento-palms, with the crabboe and haha trees dotted here and there. Amongst the hard, coarse grass of the pine-ridge, small, low spreading shrubs are found, such as *Pithecolobium ligustrum* and *Cassia diphylla;* a few ground orchids (*Habenaria* and *Stenorrhynchus*), and small, yellow-flowered hypoxids.

Of plant life in British Honduras, there is nothing which so impresses the traveller as the abundance and profusion of palms, which are everywhere seen. From the majestic cohune, which is, *par excellence*, the palm of the colony, down to the small, delicate chamædoreas, there are all gradations in size, and all variations of form and habit. Many, such as *Bactris*, are gregarious; whilst others, such as the cohune, the pimento-palm, and geonomas, are restricted to certain localities, where, however, they are fairly abundant. Close along the shore, the cultivated coco-nut is a familiar object; but not far off, forming a dense grove, and standing almost in the brackish water of a lagoon or river, may be seen the bastard or salt-water pimento-palm (*Bactris sp.*); along the banks of the rivers inland another and a taller prickly palm is abundant, known to the colonists as "Poknoboy" (*Bactris horrida*), which owes its local name to an encounter between the woodcutters and the Spaniards, in which the former used, with considerable effect, the stems of this palm as pike-handles.*

The "bay-leaf palm," which is evidently only the young

---

* This palm is sometimes known as *Pork-and-dough-boy*, the latter being the staple diet of the mahogany-cutters; hence pork-and-do-boy, and poknoboy.

form of the "bootan" (*Sabal excelsa*), is common in the broken-ridge country. Its large, fan-shaped leaves, especially in the young state, before it has formed a stem, are abundantly used for thatching purposes. The "give-and-take" (*Acanthothrinax*) is chiefly a cohune-ridge palm; it is so abundantly covered with long compound spines, about 3 to 4 inches long, that it is a very formidable object.

The cabbage-palm (*Oreodoxa oleracea*) is abundant in the lowlands, and also appears on banks of rivers in the interior, where its tall clean stem, surmounted by a canopy of feathery fronds, is a familiar landmark. *Oreodoxa regia* appears to be confined to Belize, where, probably, it is an introduced plant.

In the cohune-ridge proper, the silver-thatch (*Thrinax argentea*), big-thatch (*Sabal mexicana*), and the monkey-tail (*Euterpe edulis*) grow in cool, moist situations under the shade of tall timber-trees, where their finer habit is in marked contrast to that of the ampler and more expansive cohune. As already hinted, the supa, or gru-gru (*Acrocomia sclerocarpa*), disdains the confined air and moist soil of the forest, preferring the more exposed and drier, though poorer, situations of the broken-ridge, where its somewhat swollen and prickly grey stem towers above everything. Second only to the formidable spines of the bambu are the recurved or hooked spines of *Desmoncus*, a climbing palm, which, forming an impenetrable mass hanging from the branches of the highest trees, often bars the progress of the traveller.

Of the small palms belonging to the genera *Chamædorea* and *Geonoma* there are numerous species, forming a large percentage of the undergrowth in the cohune-ridge. One, called by the negroes "no-give-massa," from its fine twig-like stem, has evidently been used in former days for purposes of discipline not recognised at present. *Chamædorea Ernesti-Augusti*, with its partially pinnate fronds, and simple, unbranched spadix, is often not more than 3 feet high when in fruit. Other species are *C. elegans*, *C. humilis*, *C. desmoncoides*, and *C. graminifolia*. *C. tenella* is doubtfully present; but, if it were, British Honduras would possess not only the most majestic of pinnate-leaved palms, but also the smallest of known species.

To most people in the colony, as well as to their friends at home, orchids, so easily cultivated, and yet so bright and beautiful in flower, are of great interest. British Honduras cannot boast of orchids equal in profusion, in delicious fragance, and in brilliant colours, to those of New Grenada, Quito, and Peru; but in many species attractive to the eye, as well as in delicacy of fragance, the country possesses many representatives. The two commonest orchids in the colony are *Schomburgkia tibicina* and *Epidendrum bicornutum*. These cover the trunks of trees in dense masses, both along the coast, where they are exposed to the salt spray, as well as some places inland. Both have strong fleshy and somewhat hollow stems, and flower profusely. Possibly the handsomest orchid in the colony is *Brassovola Digbyana*, very common on logwood-trees in swamps in the north, but rare elsewhere. Another species (*Brassovola caudata*) is very common in the neighbourhood of Belize, and in dry places in the north. *Oncidium* and *Epidendrum*, are the more widely distributed genera; but *Gongora*, *Chysis*, *Maxillaria*, *Cycnodes*, *Catasetum*, *Mormodes*, *Coryanthes*, and *Dichœa* are also well represented. Two species of *Epidendrum* (*E. cochleatum* and *E. fuscatum*), confined chiefly to the hills in Jamaica, are found here at sea-level. Also *Pleurothallis tribuloides*, found at 4,000 feet in Jamaica, is met with at sea-level at Point Ycacos. On the stem of pimento-palms in the pine-ridges the somewhat rare and very handsome *Galeandra Baurii* flowers after the autumn rains; while hanging from the forks of the crabboe-trees are the peculiar long, insect-like tresses of *Cycnoches Egertonianum*. On a calabash-tree near Orange Walk (Old River), masses of a small *Oncidium* (not more than 2 inches in height, with flowers fully an inch in diameter) were found covering the branches and giving the tree quite a bright yellow tint. On trunks of trees in the river below the Big Falls, a fine plant of *Oncidium cebolleta* was found, as also *O. lanceanum*, in full flower. In the pine-ridges the terrestrial *Habenaria* and *Stenorrhynchus* were common.

From the abundant shade found in the cohune-ridges, as also from the abundance of water and moisture in the air and soil generally, it may be readily supposed that ferns are very widely and extensively distributed. There would appear to be only one species of tree-fern (*Alsophila*), and that chiefly confined to the south; but in such genera as *Asplenium*, *Aspidium*, *Nephrodium*, *Polypodium*, *Acrostichum*, *Cheilanthes*, *Pellæa*, *Pteris*, *Anemia*, and *Adiantum*, there are numerous and widely-distributed species. Of scandent forms, such as *Lygodium*, there are two or more species found hanging in festoons over trees on the borders of the forest. Gleichenias cover exposed banks and ridges; anemias are abundant on rocky ledges; while several handsome species of *Adiantum* (*A. tenerum*, *A. tetraphyllum*, &c.) are found in the limestone hills of the interior. With the latter, in deep shade, is *Selaginella erythropus*, carpeting the ground with its feathery, fan-shaped fronds.

It would be impossible to describe satisfactorily the rich profusion and abundance of plant life as seen in the Central American forests. Each tree, with its huge branches covered with orchids and bromeliads, and its trunk festooned with climbing aroids and tresses of ferns and club-mosses, is a botanic garden in itself. Tall, slender palm-stems, " great broad-leaved heliconiæ, leathery melastomæ, and succulent-stemmed, lop-sided, flesh-coloured begonias "—these, with the fine feathery branches of the bambu, make up a picture which can be seen and enjoyed only in tropical lands, but which can never be adequately described.

CHAPTER V.

Cacao plant. *T. angustifolia.* Shade necessary. Socunusco or Tabasco cacao. Castilloa or Central American rubber. Description of tree: leaves, flowers, and fruit. How to collect seeds. How to raise plants. How to tap trees. How to prepare the rubber. Use of juice of the moon-plant. Use of alum. Preparation of rubber ready for shipment. Yield of trees. Value. Extended use of the Castilloa tree. Shade trees in general. Superiority of Castilloa over other shade trees. Ceara rubber-tree. Soil, situation, and districts for the Castilloa. Distance apart. Pruning. Returns of cultivated trees. Vanilla plant. Found wild and in bearing. Value. Directions for cultivation. How to fertilise flowers. How to cure beans. Fibre plants. Pita and henequin. How to establish a henequin plantation. Return at the end of five or six years. Preparation of fibre. Value of the industry in Yucatan. Cockspur-tree. Tococa. Habits of ants. Provision-tree. Indigo. Arnatto. Karamani, or hog-gum. Oil of Ben. Balsam of Tolu. Balsam of Copaiba. Guaco. Corkwood. Manchineel.

ALTHOUGH the fact does not appear to be generally known, one, if not more, species of the cacao plant, producing the cacao nibs of commerce, is a native of British Honduras. In the forests along the banks of the Rio Grande and in the neighbourhood of the Toledo Settlement, and again in the forests on the western frontier, near the upper portions of the Belize River, cacao-trees are found wild in the woods, with their stems covered with flowers, and often loaded with fruit. The trees which came under my notice in the south were probably forms of the same species (*Theobroma cacao*), which yield the best kinds of Trinidad cacao; but in other instances the characters approached more nearly to *T. angustifolia*, which is supposed to be a distinct species, and under cultivation in

Guatemala. This last is no doubt the Tabasco cacao of the Atlantic slopes of Central America, which is probably identical with the celebrated Socunusco cacao of the Pacific slopes. The wild trees in the forest grow under the shade of large overhanging trees in deep soil, and in rather moist situations. That cacao-trees, even under cultivation in the plains, require permanent shade, is very clearly indicated by the circumstances under which the wild trees are found. The cacao-tree never appears to such advantage, or thrives so luxuriantly, as when it occupies a cool, moist situation, in deep, well-drained soil; thoroughly sheltered from strong winds, and with moderate shade above. The Socunusco cacao, grown in the province of that name on the Pacific, is supposed to be the best cacao known, and little, if any, of it finds its way into foreign markets. This cacao is supposed to have been reserved, from time immemorial, for the use of the Royal Court at Mexico: and the drink or beverage prepared from it was highly appreciated by the Mexicans, with whom it was held with religious veneration. As the trees have the same habit and characteristics as those of Caracas cacao, derived from the class of *Cacao criollo*, the trees in British Honduras will, no doubt, be found to be the yellow-fruited variety of that highly esteemed plant. In *Forastero cacao* (the class of cacao chiefly under cultivation in Trinidad and Grenada), the yellow varieties are supposed to yield finer and better cacao than the red; and if these characteristics obtain in the *Cacao criollo* class, then we have in the Tabasco or Socunusco cacao of Central America, which, as shown above, is also a native of British Honduras, the finest quality of cacao which can be grown.

In the woods the fruits are smaller, probably, than they would be if the trees were under cultivation; but if any difficulty were experienced in obtaining sufficient quantities of seed in British Honduras, they might be obtained from Guatemala, or from Tabasco, or any districts on the mainland known to possess this particular variety. In a subsequent chapter I shall deal, particularly, with the methods to be pursued in establishing a cacao plantation; and point out the kind of land and the localities best adapted for it.

Next to cacao, the most interesting plant found wild in the forests of British Honduras is the indiarubber-tree, called by the natives "Toonu." This tree (*Castilloa elastica*), a member of the bread-fruit family, and whose produce is known in commerce as Castilloa, or Central American rubber, should become, in course of time, one of the most important cultivated trees in the colony. The large and increasing demand which arises for indiarubber for all kinds of appliances in arts and manufactures renders the production of this article an industry of great value. The original supplies of indiarubber, derived from various trees growing wild in tropical forests all over the world, are likely, at no distant date, to fall far short of the demand; and hence these supplies will require to be supplemented, if not, indeed, to be replaced, as in the case of Cinchona barks, by the produce of trees under cultivation. The Toonu in British Honduras is found in most of the cohune ridges of the country, and especially along the banks and in the valleys bordering Mullin's River, Sittee River, and the Rio Grande, in the south; as well as along the Sibun River and the upper waters of the Belize River, in the west. The tree is very abundant in some places, although daily becoming scarcer in the immediate neighbourhood of settlements. It grows to the height of about 40 to 50 feet; has a thick, clean stem, about 2 feet in diameter at the base, and in habit of growth much resembles a bread-fruit tree, to which, indeed, as mentioned above, it is closely allied. The leaves are large, oblong in shape, and clothed, especially in the young state, with a dense coat of hairs. The flowers appear in February or March: they are monœcious—that is, have the male and female in different flowers on the same tree. The fruit, of a brownish-green colour when ripe, has very much the appearance of a raspberry flattened or depressed, about an inch in diameter; the numerous seeds being massed together and enclosed in papery capsules, covered with a brown tomentum. When taken out of the husk the seeds are of a whitish colour, about as large as castor-oil seeds, and evidently soon lose their vitality. The best way to collect the seeds, which ripen in May or June, would be to gather the fruits, just before they burst, and to spread them out for a few days under shade. When intended to be shipped, the seeds should be packed in earth and carefully fastened down.

FRUIT OF CASTILLOA ELASTICA, WITH SEED.

To establish plantations, the seeds might, in the first instance, be planted in open nurseries, or in boxes or beds, raised some 4 or 5 feet above the ground, so as to be beyond the reach of ants and mice. The plants thus raised might be transplanted at the end of twelve months, and put out in their permanent places in the field. Where, however, seed is abundant, and ants and mice are not likely to destroy them, two or three seeds might be planted out at once, "at stake" as it is called, in the same manner as recommended for cacao. In this latter case, if all three grow, one strong plant might be left, and the other two either transplanted to supply vacancies or destroyed.

The Castilloa rubber-tree is fit to be tapped for caoutchouc, or the elastic gummy substance produced by its milk, when about seven to ten years old. The milk is obtained at present from trees growing wild, by men called rubber-gatherers, who are well acquainted with all the localities inhabited by the Toonu. The proper season for tapping the trees is after the autumn rains, which occur some months after the trees have ripened their fruit, and before they put forth buds for the next season. The flow of milk is most copious during the months of October, November, December, and January. The rubber-gatherers commence operations on an untapped tree by reaching with a ladder, or by means of lianes, or tie-ties, the upper portions of its trunk, and scoring the bark the whole length with deep cuts, which extend all round. The cuts are sometimes made so as to form a series of spirals all round the tree; at other times they are shaped simply like the letter V, with a small piece of hoop-iron, the blade of a cutlass, or the leaf of a palm placed at the lower angle to form a spout to lead the milk into a receptacle below. A number of trees are treated in this manner, and left to bleed for several hours. At the close of the day, the rubber-gatherer collects all the milk, washes it by means of water, and leaves it standing till the next morning. He now procures a quantity of the stem of the moon-plant (*Calonictyon speciosum*), pounds it into a mass, and throws it into a bucket of water. After this decoction has been strained, it is added to the rubber-milk, in the proportion of one pint to a gallon, or until, after brisk stirring, the whole of the milk is coagulated. The masses of rubber floating on the surface are now strained from the liquid, kneaded into cakes, and placed under heavy weights to get rid of all watery particles. When perfectly drained and dry, the rubber cakes are fit for the market, and exported generally in casks. In Spanish Honduras, and other places in Central

America, instead of the juice of the moon-plant, a solution of alum is used to coagulate the milk; but it is said that the injudicious use of alum tends to make the rubber hard and brittle, and to depreciate its value. As, however, it is desirable to place both methods before planters, in order to lead them to carry on experiments, and to prepare the rubber in the most economical and expeditious manner possible, I quote the following, which appeared in the columns of the *Colonial Guardian*, published at Belize :—

"EXTRACTION AND PREPARATION OF INDIARUBBER.—The milk of the indiarubber-tree is obtained by making longitudinal incisions on the bark. It must then be strained through a fine sieve to free it from minute portions of wood and other impurities, and placed into a cask standing upright. After remaining for a short time in this receptacle, a quantity of rain or spring water, double the quantity of the rubber milk, is to be added thereto, and strained through a piece of brown cotton into another cask. More water—equal in quantity to that already added—should be thrown into the cask, so that there should be four parts of water to one of rubber milk. This mixture is to be allowed to remain in that cask twenty-four hours, after which the indiarubber floats at the top of the liquid. The water may then be carefully drawn off by removing the spigot from the lower end of the cask, and watching to stop the flow as soon as any indiarubber begins to pass. This is easily ascertained by observing, accompanying the blackish water which flows from the cask, small, long, and thin threads of rubber.

"When all the dirty water shall have been removed from the cask, other four parts of clean water to one of the rubber are to be again added, and after twenty-four hours the same operation is to be gone through with. The remaining liquid should then be placed in small receptacles, with little spigots through which the remaining water is then to be drawn off. After this, add to every 100 pounds of the now purified rubber milk a pint bottle full of a solution containing one ounce of alum dissolved in hot water.

"The new rubber must be well stirred; and as fast as coagulated lumps appear, they are to be carefully removed from the liquid and shaped into a ball; this is to be then put in a press and all the remaining water squeezed out of it. After being removed from the press the rubber is to be placed in the shade, to await its turn for being packed up, to be sent to a foreign market."

A large tree of Castilloa, say 2 feet in diameter, is said to yield eight gallons of milk when first cut. Each gallon of milk, in the proper season, will make about two pounds of rubber. Hence a tree of this size will give a return of sixteen pounds of rubber, of the value of $10.

In British Honduras, the rubber-gatherers are supposed to require a license before they can tap trees on Government lands; but, practically, there are no restrictions placed upon them, and trees of all ages and sizes are ruthlessly bled, many of which, I fear, never recover. While in the colony I was fortunate enough to meet with an intelligent rubber-gatherer, on Mullin's River, with whom I spent some time, making observations on the habitats and characteristic of the trees, as well as the methods pursued in tapping them. A fine piece of rubber, prepared by this man with the use of the juice of the *Calonictyon*, was brought away with me, and is now deposited in the museum of the Royal Gardens, Kew.

Having thus described the Castilloa rubber-tree and its use, I would now mention that this tree, which grows very fast, and gives a safe and sure return, is capable of being rendered of the greatest value to planters, not only in this colony, but everywhere in connection with the cultivation of bananas, cacao, Liberian coffee, oranges, and other shade-loving plants. In most countries, planters are obliged to have permanent shade-trees for their plantations; and generally the trees used are worthless except as shade-trees. For instance, in Trinidad the recognised shade-tree for cacao is the "immortelle" (*Erythrina umbrosa*), a tree whose only merits are that it is a rapid grower, and very common in the districts suitable for cacao. The wood, however, is so brittle that large branches, or even trees, are broken off in strong winds, causing serious havoc among the cacao: this tree is also a surface feeder, and sends its long sinuous roots all through the plantation, robbing the cacao-trees of the sustenance which they so much require. The planters in Trinidad are, therefore, gradually discarding the immortelle as a shade-tree, and adopting others more suitable. In other places, the trumpet-tree (*Cecropia peltata*) is used to shade cacao and coffee, whilst some adopt the jack-fruit tree, the hog-plum, or the rain-tree (*Pithecolobium saman*). Neither of these trees can, however, compare with the Castilloa rubber, either in quickness of growth, in shade-giving properties, or in the return which it is likely to give the planter, year after year, if properly treated. Hence this Central America rubber combines all the conditions desired in a tropical shade-tree, and on this account deserves the earnest attention, not only of planters, but of all those who have it in their power to extend or promote its cultivation throughout our tropical possessions.

As I mentioned before, supplies of indiarubber are, year by year, falling short of the demand; and it will soon become a serious question where we are to obtain the immense quantities of this important vegetable product which has become so essential an element in all our industries. This subject has received some attention; and Mr. Clements Markham, who did so much to introduce the quinine-yielding plants to India, has also advocated the extended cultivation of rubber-plants. The authorities at the Royal Gardens, Kew, with their accustomed interest in the welfare of our colonial possessions, have procured rubber seeds and plants, and distributed them far and wide, for the purpose of establishing them under cultivation; but many of the rubber-plants thus distributed are not such as can be easily cultivated under ordinary circumstances. For instance, the Para-rubber (*Hevea brasiliensis*) will only grow in swamps or estuarine banks, places quite unsuitable for an European to live in. The Landolphias, and other shrubby climbers, require such special conditions and attention that I fear they will not commend themselves for general adoption. The true india-rubber-trees (*Ficus elastica*) and their allies do not appear to thrive and yield commercial rubber except in Burmah and other warm, steamy countries, and they are seldom planted elsewhere, except as ornamental shade-trees. There remain, therefore, only two important rubber-plants on our list, and these are the Ceara rubber-tree (*Manihot Glaziovi*), yielding the Ceara scrap of South America, and the subject under notice, viz., the Castilloa rubber-tree of Central America. The Ceara rubber-tree, being a spurge-wort (*Euphorbiaceæ*), has a tendency to form large tuberous roots, almost like those of the Cassava plant, and these, being near the surface, tend to impoverish the soil and destroy any hopes of growing other plants near it. This tree, also, does not become large enough, nor strong enough, to afford high shade for cacao-trees: and lastly, the rubber is not so abundant, nor does it command such high prices, as that derived from the Castilloa tree. Hence, under these circumstances, I am led to recommend, very strongly, the adoption of this Central American rubber, as the best tree for all tropical plants requiring shade, and also as the best rubber-tree, which, all round, offers the most favourable inducements to the planter to undertake its cultivation. The Castilloa tree grows in deep loamy or sandy soil, is a deep feeder, striking its roots far into the ground, and not exhausting the surface soil; again, it grows with wonderful rapidity, soon forming a large, handsome shade-tree; and lastly, it gives a return in rubber within eight or ten years, when most other trees do not mature for some twenty or thirty years.

In a cacao plantation, the rubber-trees may be planted at 40 feet apart, or one tree between every third tree of cacao. When young the lower branches fall off naturally, and by a little subsequent trimming and pruning the trees might be so trained as to give the requisite shelter and shade, while at the same time there is a clean stem for facilitating the extraction of the rubber.

If rubber-trees are planted in cultivated areas, as shade-trees for cacao, Liberian coffee, oranges, &c., as mentioned above, the return from them at the end of eight or ten years would average, at least, about £1 sterling per tree, or at the rate of £25 per acre. This return might be repeated in about five years by the same trees, and continued, at certain intervals, as long as the trees lasted.

The Vanilla plant (*Vanilla planifolia*) is also a native of British Honduras; and fine masses of it are found in the forest, hanging down from the trees, which, when the fruit is ripe, diffuses a fragrance perceptible at a considerable distance. If only these pods were gathered "when full," as planters term it, that is, before they begin to turn yellow, and properly cured, a considerable trade might be made in them. Being an orchid, the flowers of the vanilla have a wonderful appliance, which requires the presence of an insect to fertilise them. That this insect is present in British Honduras is abundantly proved by the numbers of bunches found on the wild plants. At present these bunches are simply allowed to rot on the vines and run to waste. Vanilla is a valuable spice, which in some countries, as in the Isle of Bourbon, where it has been successfully introduced and cultivated, forms a valuable article of export. Well-cured vanilla-pods fetch as high as 30s. per pound. The following directions for establishing vanilla from cuttings, and curing the pods, have been lately published by the Botanical Department, Jamacia; and I quote them as applicable, in every respect, to the circumstances of British Honduras:—

"VANILLA.—This is a vigorous, soft-stemmed vine, the cured fruits of which are the valuable vanilla-beans of commerce. If cuttings are taken, their upper ends, or portion to appear above ground, may be readily determined by examination of the base of the attached leaf, in the axil or upper face of which is a small growth-bud.

"Cut the stem with, say, three or four joints, at one-fourth of an inch below the basal node or joint; then place the base of each cutting shallowly in prepared soil, against the bole or trunk of a rough-barked, low-branching tree, as, for instance, calabash; or on a low-trellised frame 3 to 4 feet high, the supports of which should be unbarked logwood, yoke or calabash.

"If the insect which fertilises the flowers of this orchid, in its natural habitat, is not present, in order to secure a crop of fruit it is necessary that the flowers should be artificially fertilised. This may be easily accomplished as follows:

"In the flower is a central white column, at the summit of which is a detachable cap or anther, which if touched on the lower front edge with a sharpened pencil or knife blade will adhere to the implement. The pollen masses contained in the anther must then be made to lightly touch the viscous (sticky) disk situated on the front of the column. Each flower must be so treated at or about noon of the day on which it opens.

"To cure vanilla-beans gather when full: steep for about two minutes in boiling water and place in flannel to dry in the sun. When perfectly dry, place them the next day on plates of iron or tin, anointing once or twice with sweet oil, to keep them soft and plump. Complete the curing process by exposing them carefully in the sun for several days. When quite cured they should have a uniformly rich brown colour, and the full fragrance of this valuable product."

Of plants yielding fibre there are two, natives of British Honduras, which are cultivated to a great extent in other countries, and in no country more successfully than in the Mexican State of Yucatan, on the northern frontier. The first of these fibre-plants is the pita, or silk grass (*Bromelia pita*), abundant in the forests in the west, where it covers extensive tracts of country. The other plant is the sisal hemp, or henequin (*Agave ixtli*), the fibre of which is exported from Yucatan to the annual value of £100,000.

Both these plants might be cultivated on the land in the northern territory, and Corosal might become the centre of a large fibre industry. A henequin plantation might be established even in dry, poor soils, unsuited for anything else, and bring a large return on the outlay. The Agave is easily propagated by root-suckers, which are removed from the parent plant when about 18 inches high. They take about five or six years to mature, and after that period the leaves may be cut twice a year for twenty years, each cutting yielding about fifteen leaves per plant. The preparation of the fibre is accomplished by means of a very simple machine obtained from the United States, which removes the pulp and cleans the fibre at the rate of one leaf per minute. After passing through the machine the fibre is simply dried in the sun, and then baled ready for shipment. The *Textile Record* (American) states that the "essence of the henequin trade is its certain and abundant profit. The fibre costs the planter, by the time that he has it in the bale, about two-thirds of a cent per pound. The freight charge per pound to New York is three-quarters of a cent. Adding commissions and incidental expenses, the total charge on each pound sold is close upon one-and-a-half cent, and the selling price per pound is from five to seven cents. In the English market the price of sisal hemp is about £30 per ton."

In the neighbourhood of the settlements in the south a common tree is the "cockspur" (*Acacia spadicifera*), which derives its name from the fact of its being armed with formidable curved spines, about 2 inches long, produced in pairs at the base of each branch and leaf. The spines on examination are found to be hollow, and probably have been excavated by a colony of small ants which have established themselves there. Critically noticed, a small aperture is seen on the side near one end of a horn, through which the ants pass in and out. The other horn, although hollow, has no aperture on the outside, and as the inside partition between the two horns has been removed the ants have snug and safe quarters which can be very easily defended. During the wet season all these horns are filled with ants, which keep guard over every portion of the plant, and especially against the aggressions of the leaf-cutting ants. As the "cockspur," being an acacia, has numerous glands frequented by the ants, they are not only securely housed but are provided with a bountiful supply of food. Another plant which is used by ants for nests is *Tococa coriacea*, a common Melastomad in the neighbourhood of Belize. The leaf-stalks below have a kind of bladder or pouch attached to them, divided longitudinally into two compartments. The ants avail themselves of these cavities and utilise them, as in the case of the hollow processes of the cockspur, as nests. It is remarkable how regularly and consistently the glands of the tococa and their colony of small black ants are associated together. Every pouch on every plant that was seen was occupied by ants, and "if the leaf was shaken ever so little, they would rush out and scour all over it in search of the aggressor."

The Provision-tree (*Pachira aquatica*) is a common object along river banks and moist places: the fruit is round, about the size of a child's head, and contains numerous large chestnut-like seeds, sometimes used for food by the natives, during times of scarcity.

Indigo (*Indigofera anil*) appears to be indigenous to the colony, and widely distributed. Its cultivation does not, however, offer any hope of becoming at present a remunerative industry, owing to the competition of the numerous aniline and other artificial dyes obtained from coal-tar.

The Arnatto (*Bixa orellana*) grows freely near the settlements, and its seeds, which yield an orange or yellow dye for silks and for staining cheese, might easily become an article of export. Near Regalia Estate I noticed a handsome-foliaged tree covered with red flower-buds, known locally as "waika," or chewstick. This tree (*Symphonia globulifera*) is the source of Karamani resin (Hog-gum of Jamaica) which in British Guiana is collected from among the roots of old trees. It is of medicinal value, besides being in demand in the arts. The supple-jacks, or tie-ties, common in the woods, include *Paullinia sorbilis*, the pounded seeds of which yield the Guarana bread of Brazil. This bread is sold in the form of rolls or sticks, and used both as food and medicine. The horse-radish tree (*Moringa pterygosperma*) is naturalised in the neighbourhood of Belize; the young seed pods are sometimes used as a vegetable in curries, or pickled. The root is pungent like horse-radish, and properly prepared may be used as a vesicant. The oil abundantly derived from the seeds, although good, does not appear to be so valuable as that derived from another species (*M. aptera*), which is said to yield the true oil of Ben. Amongst trees of medicinal value that yielding Balsam of Tolu (*Myroxylon Toluifera*) deserves special mention. It is a large handsome tree found in the interior, which yields, by incision into the wood, a balsam used in medicine as an expectorant and stimulant. "Tolu lozenges are well known as a remedy in allaying coughs." Balsam of Copaiba is yielded by several species of Copaifera, one of which, probably *C. officinalis*, is native of British Honduras. The balsam as it flows from the trees is very thin and colourless, but soon becomes thicker and assumes a yellow tint.

The Guaco (*Mikania guaco*), a composite twiner with cordate leaves and large panicles of pale lavender-coloured flowers, is one of the commonest plants on the outskirts of woods and along road-sides; the leaves are used as a febrifuge and anthelmintic, but the chief interest connected with the plant is on account of its being supposed to be a powerful antidote for the bite of venomous serpents. "So strong is the impression of the powerful medicinal virtue possessed by guaco that no Indian ever traverses the dark and dense forests without carrying a portion of it in his pouch."[*] The Naseberry or bully-trees, as noticed before, are abundant in the forests: and from one, if not more, an elastic gum is furnished which is imported into New York from Mexico, under the name of Chicle gum, for use as a masticatory.

The Fustic (*Maclura aurantiaca*) is one of the most valuable trees of Central America, as its timber yields a yellow dye.

The Corkwood, or alligator-apple (*Anona palustris*), bears a

---

[*] See "Journal of the Society of Arts," January 11th, 1857.

narcotic and probably a poisonous fruit, very similar to the Sweet-sop, which should be carefully avoided. It is said to be eaten by alligators as it drops [into the water, and hence its name. The wood, which is known as corkwood, is used for lining boxes, stopping bottles, &c. From the Zamia, or "bulrush," so abundant along the sea-shore and banks of rivers, a starch, similar to what is known as wild sago starch in the West Indies, might be made in considerable quantities. Among the forest-trees one bearing acacia-like leaves, and rough, leathery moniliform pods, probably a species of *Piptadenia*, is of interest on account of the use to which the seeds are sometimes applied by the Indians. After being roasted they are pounded and mixed with powdered lime, and made into a kind of snuff which is said to produce "a peculiar kind of intoxication, almost amounting to frenzy." Reference has been made above to the poisonous qualities of the alligator apple, but these are as nothing compared with those of the Manchineel or Manzanillo-tree, so common in the West Indian Islands—hence the town of Manchioneal in Jamaica—and in most parts of Central America.

In British Honduras the Manchineel (*Hippomane Mancinella*) is confined to dry ridges near the sea-shore, and it is by no means a common tree. "The virulent nature of the juice of the Manchineel-tree has given rise, in the Western Hemisphere, to nearly as wonderful stories as those associated with the upas tree in the Eastern." Admitting that its virulent powers have been exaggerated, there can be no doubt, however, that the juice exuded by this member of the spurge worts (*Euphorbiaceæ*) possesses a considerable amount of acridity: and it is capable of producing very painful if not deadly symptoms, if incautiously brought into contact with cut surfaces, or taken into the system. (See also Dr. Seeman's Narrative of the Voyage of H.M.S. "Herald.")

The Carapa (*C. quianensis*), possibly an introduced tree, possesses a large fruit, containing numerous oily seeds, which eventually split into five pieces. The bark is said to be used as a febrifuge. The timber, known in Guiana as crabwood, is in request for cabinet-making and for masts and spars of vessels. By pressure the seeds yield a liquid oil, known as carap-oil or crab-oil, suitable for burning in lamps. Another tree whose bark is supposed to possess febrifugal properties was brought to my notice by Mr. Fowler, who described it in the following words:—" This tree, called by the Indians Capoche, appears to be the natural cinchona of this country, for it is used for fevers and has a bitter taste. The tree is very scarce. The Indians make cups from the wood for the purpose of water being steeped in them, which is given to children for fever and also as an anthelmintic. There is another tree, called Cromanty, more common; the bark is thicker and has the same characteristics, but is not so highly prized as the capoche." Unfortunately, so far, no flowers or fruit of this latter tree, which is probably a member of the *Lauraceæ*, have been obtained. Another plant mentioned by Mr. Fowler, a tie-tie, or vine (*Menispermaceæ*), is used by the Indians to stupefy fish. They pound it in a mortar, dam up a pool and then throw the pounded mass into the water. In a short time any fish in the pool come to the surface in an unconscious state, and so are easily caught. It is much to be desired that good specimens, including flowers and fruit, of these and many other plants known to be used by the natives of Central America, be forwarded for identification, and that the specimens be accompanied by full and clear descriptions of the purposes to which they are applied.

CHAPTER VI.

Sugar-cane cultivation. Its introduction. Cost of production. Causes of decline of sugar industry. How to be revived. Muscavado sugar. New varieties of canes to be introduced. Banana cultivation. Hints to cultivators. Abundant land for bananas. Present position of the industry. Cacao. Advantages possessed by British Honduras. Nature of land. How to start a plantation. Shade plants required. India-rubber-tree. Liberian coffee. Market value in America. Topping and pruning. Pulping machines. Oranges, limes, and lemons. Coco-nuts: prolific yield. How to plant. Planting distances. Cost of plantations. Export trade. Rice. Indian corn. Tobacco. Pine-apples, how to cultivate. Cinchona.

AMONG the most important plants now under cultivation in the colony, possibly sugar-cane, bananas, and coco-nuts take the leading place.

The present position of sugar-cane cultivation may not compare favourably with what it was a few years ago, both the number of estates, as well as the area actually under canes, having greatly diminished. According to Mr. Fowler, "The cultivation of the sugar-cane was introduced into the colony by the Yucatecans, in 1848, who crossed the border on being expelled by the Indians from the southern part of Yucatan. The success they achieved was remarkable, and the northern district of the colony became the scene of many small flourishing plantations. The American Civil War caused some Southern planters to become settlers in the colony, and the attention of proprietors in the colony was drawn to the subject, when a large amount of capital was embarked in sugar plantations.

"Twelve large estates were started, involving an outlay of capital of £300,000. Only five are now in working order, and two of the largest of these are in the market.

"Reliable experience proves that sugar can be easily produced here for about £10 per ton, and at the rate of two tons to the acre. One planter informs me that on actual experiment one acre of picked canes yielded four tons of drained sugar. No artificial manure is required, nor any drainage, beyond mere surface drains, and hardly any cultivation beyond a couple of ploughings to clean the canes. Canes ratoon for ten or twelve years without deterioration, and instances have been quoted to me of some cut for this year's crop that have been ratooning for twenty years. From all I have been able to gather on the subject I think it can be demonstrated that well-managed estates in the colony have been able to pay their way, and persons judiciously managing their own estates have been able to make a good general living out of them, besides adding to a reserve fund, or reimbursing a fair portion of the purchase-money, within a very short time, even under recent adverse circumstances affecting the sugar trade. Whether estates can be continued with the same results will of course depend upon the state of the market, and steps taken to counteract the operation of sugar bounties, without which it is considered by those most competent to judge it will be impossible to grow sugar to a profit in any British colony."

Possibly one of the chief causes of the decline of sugar estates in this colony, is attributable to the uncertainty of the labour supply, and to the competition which must ensue (in years when mahogany and logwood are fetching remunerative prices) between mahogany cutters and the planters.

When mahogany and logwood are commanding higher prices the greater proportion of the available labour supply of the colony can easily be drawn off from the estates by the higher wages offered on mahogany works.

If the suggestions offered by me under the head of labour supply are adopted, and East India coolies are systematically introduced by Government, there can be no hindrance to the regular working of sugar estates on account of the competition of mahogany works. Coolies are unfitted for the heavy work of mahogany and logwood cutting, and consequently the whole of this class of labour will be available for the planter.

In connection with the class of sugars exported from the colony it might be found an advantage to make Muscavado rather than concrete sugar, as the demand for the former is more extensive and more regular.

With regard to the cultivation, I would suggest that a regular supply of new canes be introduced to the colony, as the continual culture of the same kind on the same land must, in time, result in a deteriorated plant, with a lower yield per acre.

At present it would appear that the Bourbon cane is exclusively cultivated.

As in all other sugar-producing colonies, with varying conditions of soil and climate, it may naturally be expected that more than one variety of cane is required to enable the planter to obtain the best results with the means at his command. I have every confidence that the establishment of nurseries of new canes, such as the Lahina of the Sandwich Islands, the Salangore, the ribbon and Java cane of Louisiana, and numerous other rich and hardy canes, would afford planters an opportunity for testing their merits, and of, eventually, greatly increasing the returns of their plantations.

As far as I could judge of the quality and nature of the soil, there is no reason to doubt that sugar-cane cultivation will be as profitable in British Honduras as in any other British colony.

For success, it is necessary to observe, as I have mentioned above, that the labour supply is adequate to the wants of the planter; that good and popular classes of sugar are made, and that judicious and systematic management is combined with high culture of canes, suitable to the nature and character of the soil and climate of each district.

The exports for 1881 in connection with this industry included 3,577 gallons of rum, of the estimated value of £665 16s.; and 1,902 tons of sugar, of the value of £37,836. The present area under canes is estimated at 2,300 acres.

Bananas.—Owing to the regular fortnightly communication by mail steamer between British Honduras and New Orleans, a large demand has arisen for bananas, coco-nuts, oranges, pine-apples, and various other fruits for the American market. At present, next to sugar, bananas would appear to be occupying chief attention in the colony, and provided a convenient and regular market is found for the produce, planters have every prospect of finding the cultivation a profitable one.

The chief points to which I would draw attention in connection with the cultivation of bananas are:—

1. That bananas should only be cultivated on rich, deep, loamy soils, in well-sheltered situations, and within easy reach of shipping facilities.

2. That on virgin soil, as indicated in the last paragraph, the plants should not be placed closer than 18 or 20 feet each way: due regard being had to the character of the plants to follow the bananas, viz., whether cacao, Liberian coffee, oranges, lemons, coco-nuts, &c.

3. That when the stools have ratooned heavily and produced, say at the end of the third year, some eight to ten stems, only four or five of these should be left to produce fruit, the remainder being cut high up or bent down so as not to cause excessive

bleeding from the stool: this treatment will result in keeping the stool in good vigorous state of health and tend to produce large saleable bunches.

4. That as soon as possible, and especially after the stools have borne a crop or two, careful moulding of the stools with manure, rich surface soil and decayed stems, will tend to keep them bearing for a longer period, and save the exhaustion which must follow heavy cropping.

The profits on banana cultivation would appear to range from £12 to £15 per acre, after the lapse of eighteen months. The cost of establishing a plantation, including the price of land (at a dollar an acre), will not exceed some £8 per acre until the first crop is reaped.

As I have already mentioned, there are some thousands of acres of splendid land suitable for banana culture in this colony, which offer every inducement to experienced tropical planters to settle down and reap the returns which must inevitably attend the judicious and careful culture of this fruit. Practically, the export trade in bananas has arisen since steam communication was established with America. The export in 1880 was 8,958 bunches of bananas, of the value of £700; in the next year, namely, 1881, it had risen to 22,229 bunches, of the estimated value of £1,469.

Cacao.—Independently of the profits arising from the cultivation of bananas themselves, the planter has other inducements before him, which must always be borne in mind in case the present demand for bananas fails, or communication with the United States becomes irregular or is completely cut off. I., for instance, some of the profits arising from the sale of bananas, and the shade they afford, are judiciously utilised for establishing plants of cacao, Liberian coffee, coco-nuts, oranges, lemons, &c., the value of the land will be considerably increased; and if at

H

any time the bananas fail (as I believe they must eventually, in even the best lands, after the lapse of a few years), the planter will have his cacao or other plants well established, and he will be independent of the precariousness of a market or regular steam communication, and find himself with a permanent cultivation yielding regular crops of an article in demand all the world over.

These remarks apply more especially to cacao than any other plant.

For detailed particulars respecting the cultivation of this plant I would commend planters to a little pamphlet prepared for the Government of Jamaica, which gives such plain and practical hints on the subject that I need not dwell upon them here.*

It may be accepted as a statement of general application that where bananas will grow and thrive, cacao will probably do the same. In other words, land that will grow bananas well, is almost sure to grow cacao well also.

To this I might add for British Honduras, that where cacao grows wild in the woods, and thrives without any care and attention, it is much more likely to thrive where it has good soil, free from competition with other plants, and where everything is done to give it the sole strength and richness of the soil.

The cacao seeds, or plants, as the case may be, on an established banana plantation, should be planted exactly midway between the stools of the bananas, so that they will ultimately stand at about 16 to 18 feet apart. If seeds are planted, the ground should first be dug deeply in spaces about 18 inches in

---

* "Cacao: How to Grow and How to Cure it." London: S. W. Silver & Co., 67, Cornhill.

diameter, and three cacao seeds planted at equal distances of not less than 8 inches apart (at the apices of an equilateral triangle), and covered with about an inch of fine rich leaf-mould, or very fine friable soil. To keep the soil cool and moist a little banana trash may be placed over the spot till the seeds have germinated. Care should be taken not to plant the seeds too deeply nor to cover them with hard, clayey soil. In such cases there is great danger of the seeds rotting in the ground before germination. If the seeds are fresh and good, they ought to show above ground in about seven or eight days.

When the seedlings treated above, have grown to about 8 inches high and developed four or five leaves, the strongest may be left in its place; the other one or two, as the case may be, can be transplanted to supply vacancies, or to plant up other portions of the plantation.

As the cacao-trees grow up, the bananas should be gradually thinned year by year, so as, eventually, to leave the plantations fully established with the cacao plants.

In addition to the shade of the bananas it may be necessary for the young seedlings to have some other shade.

About the same time that the cacao seeds are planted, seeds of chillies, stems of cassava, or some other shade plants, should be put close around them, so as to shelter the young plants in case the banana shade does not fully cover them.

Again, for permanent shade for the cacao trees when fully grown, it is customary in some places to plant some large trees such as the guango, hog-plum, trumpet-tree, &c. These are generally necessary in hot lowland districts, and no cacao walks can be said to be complete without them.

In British Honduras I would recommend for a permanent shade-tree the free use of the "Toonu," or rubber-tree (*Castilloa elastica*), already described. Seeds of these trees should be planted at the same time, or, if possible, before the cacao, and so arranged that a shade-tree will come in between every third cacao-tree.

A cacao plantation should be in full bearing about the seventh year. After that, its management is simple and easy, and requires less labour than almost any other cultivation of equal value.

Liberian Coffee.—As for cacao, so with this important low-country plant, it is very desirable to plant it at first under the shade of bananas. This large-beaned coffee is a native of the West Coast of Africa, and its chief economic value is based on the fact that it will grow in the plains at sea-level, where the preliminary expenses in the acquisition and clearing of land are naturally much lower than in the interior, where also labour is cheaper and more plentiful, and where the difficulties and expenses of transport are considerably reduced. These characteristics give Liberian coffee advantages not only over its congener the Arabian coffee, but also over almost any cultivation requiring the same capital and attention.

The market value of Liberian coffee is not so high as some of the best classes of Arabian coffee. The last sales of this coffee in the American market have realised 90s. per cwt. This, as compared with 100s. to 120s. (or even, for the best Jamaica coffee, 140s.) per cwt., does not necessarily involve a lower return for the planter. From the adaptability of the Liberian coffee to cultivation in the plains, and from its more robust and prolific character, and from the generally more economic treatment to which it is amenable, it is quite possible that its cultivation will prove even more remunerative than the high-priced varieties of the Arabian coffee.

Again, the fact that the American market is so favourable to this large-beaned and prolific coffee, gives its cultivation in

British Honduras all the aspects of a thoroughly sound investment.

With regard to establishing plantations of this coffee, the same steps may be taken as for cacao, with the exception that the Liberian coffee-trees may be placed at 10 feet apart, each way.

They may be "topped," to keep them within reach of pruners and pickers of crop, at about 5 feet 6 inches. By "topping" the trees are encouraged to throw out strong lateral branches (primaries); but owing to the height at which the first primaries of Liberian coffee are thrown out, it is evidently not advisable to top too low.

With regard to pruning Liberian coffee, the same general principles apply to it as to the Arabian coffee.

The several portions of the tree cannot have too much air and light, and a system of pruning that will remove useless growths (gormandisers), and direct the energies of the plant to the production of fruit, must be, in the end, most beneficial and successful.

Trees of Liberian coffee come into bearing in the third year; crops of at the rate of about 3 or 4 cwt. per acre should be gathered in the fifth year, with a maximum return from the tenth year.

For pulping Liberian coffee a very useful hand-pulper has been especially invented by Messrs. John Walker & Co., Colombo, Ceylon. It is said to pulp at the rate of ten bushels per hour, and to cost, complete, £18.

Another machine adapted for hulling this coffee in the "cracknel" state, that is, after the cherries have been simply dried in the sun (without pulping), is highly recommended by Mr. E. S. Morris, of Philadelphia, who has taken a great personal interest in the development of the coffee industry amongst the negroes of the Liberian Republic.

If the hulling machine were adopted, there would be no necessity for the use of water or for expensive works, and much time would be saved in the preparation of the coffee for the market.

Oranges, Limes, and Lemons.—Next to bananas, these fruits are in regular demand for the American market, and they may be cultivated in the same land as bananas with great facility. These plants do not, however, require much shade; in fact, when too much shaded by bananas, they become weak and sickly, and seldom mature into heavy-bearing trees. Oranges should be put out at about 20 feet apart. Plants may be conveniently raised from seed in boxes or beds raised some 4 or 5 feet above ground, so as to be beyond the reach of ants, rats, mice, and other noxious animals, so common in tropical countries.

The export of oranges from Jamaica, chiefly to the United States, during the year 1882, amounted to more than thirty millions, of the estimated value of £33,700.

Coco-nuts.—As already mentioned in the account of my visit to the southern settlements, many plantations of coco-nuts are being established in the colony; but there is no reason why the whole of the sea-board of British Honduras should not be covered by extensive groves of this valuable and hardy palm. The general appearance and prolific character of the trees which came under my observation in the neighbourhood of Belize, on the outer cays, and near the southern settlements, surpass anything I have ever seen. I was informed by an experienced planter that trees in good condition come into bearing in the fourth year, that they bear heavily at the sixth and seventh years, and that a good coco-nut palm in bearing in British Honduras is of the annual value of $3.

Many of the trees noticed near the settlements had evidently, when young, been simply placed on the surface, and not planted deep down where the roots could have firm hold of the ground: hence they were leaning over against each other, and many had been completely overthrown by strong winds.

In hot, sandy soils, young coco-nut plants should be placed in holes (at the bottom of an inverted cone) 3 feet wide and 3 feet deep in the centre; if possible, a small quantity of manure or good surface soil should be mixed with the sand and placed at the bottom of the pit. If the weather is very dry, the young plants require to be well "mulched," *i.e.*, covered round with trash, vegetable *débris*, or leaf-mould, and regularly watered until they are fully established.

Where the soil is deep and rich, and the land cool, the same care and attention are not absolutely necessary, but in every case I would recommend that the young plants be placed in holes sufficiently deep to allow the roots to have firm hold of the ground, and thus be able to withstand strong winds.

With regard to the distances at which coco-nuts should be planted, due regard must be had to the character of the soil and the probable growth of the trees.

It is better to plant too widely than too closely. Distances of say 21 feet are much too close for British Honduras, and as a rule it would be better to fix the distance at 28 to 30 feet for average soils, and 33 feet (half a chain) for rich, good soils.

Where trees are planted too closely, they are drawn up into long feeble stems, and bear poor crops, the individual nuts being small and light. The mistake of too close planting can only be rectified by taking out every other tree, when, again, they will stand at such wide distances apart, that a great portion of the land will be wasted.

A coco-nut plantation in Jamaica, well established and in full bearing (say at the end of eight years with sixty trees to the acre), may be safely assumed to be worth at the rate of £10 per acre.

The cost of establishing a coco-nut plantation in that island, including all expenses until it comes into bearing, do not amount to more than £8 per acre.

The export of coco-nuts from Jamaica, and chiefly for the United States, in 1880, reached a maximum of over six million nuts. These were of an estimated value of £20,000.

With regular steam communication with America, there is no doubt that all the coco-nuts that could be grown in British Honduras, would find a ready market in the States. At the time of my visit as much as $28 per thousand were offered for coco-nuts on the spot, by the mail steamer·; none, however, could be had, and the steamer had to return to New Orleans practically empty; in fact, neither bananas, oranges, nor coco-nuts could be had to the extent required.

The export of coco-nuts from British Honduras for the last six years has shown a remarkable development, and is as follows:—

1876	381,000.
1877	604,000.
1878	698,000.
1879	919,000.
1880	1,623,000.
1881	6,047,160.

The values of the shipments in 1881 are placed at £6,047 16s.

Rice.—Although upland rice is grown to some extent in the colony, and about 240 acres are returned as under this cultivation, there is no doubt a much larger area, especially in all logwood districts, could be placed under this important cereal. With the increase in the number of cooly labourers, the local demand for rice must exceed the supply; indeed, at the present time, rice is being imported to the extent of some two thousand bags. If it is accepted as an axiom that "wherever mahogany will grow, there every tropical product will flourish, and wherever logwood grows there you can produce the finest rice," then British Honduras should produce rice, not merely enough for its own wants, but to supply the whole of the West Indian Islands.

Indian Corn.—Maize (*Zea mays*), or Indian corn, may be looked upon as the staple food of the Indians and Caribs, who make it into *tortillas*, or thin cakes baked upon gridles. The cultivation of maize is probably one of the oldest upon the American continent, the Indians having been found engaged in it at the period when the New World was discovered.*

Combined with bananas and plantains, or as a catch crop with oranges, cacao, and other plants of a permanent character, maize may be grown to a very large extent.

Although some 7,000 acres are returned as under cultivation of maize, the whole of the produce is consumed in the colony, none being at present exported.

---

* "In Central America, the bread made from the maize is prepared, at the present day, exactly as it was in ancient Mexico. The grain is first of all boiled along with wood ashes, or a little lime; the alkali loosens the outer skin of the grain, and this is rubbed off with the hands in running water; a little of it at a time is placed upon a slightly concave stone, called a *metlate*, from the Aztéc *metlatl*, on which it is rubbed with another stone, shaped like a rolling-pin. A little water is thrown on it, as it is bruised, and it is thus formed into paste. A ball of the paste is taken and flattened out, between the hands, into a cake about 10 inches diameter, and $\frac{1}{10}$ inch thick, which is baked on a slightly concave earthenware pan. The cakes so made are called *tortillas*, and are very nutritious. When travelling, I preferred them myself to bread made from wheaten flour. When well made and eaten warm, they are very palatable."—*The Naturalist in Nicaragua*, p. 56.

Tobacco.—Tobacco is raised in small quantities by Indians and Caribs, but not nearly sufficient to meet the demands of the colony. In 1880, 62,004 pounds of tobacco were imported for local consumption.

The introduction of the best kinds of Havana tobacco seed from Cuba, and the settlement of a few Cubans, would no doubt give this cultivation an important impulse.

The light fine soils along banks of rivers are admirably adapted for tobacco, which, if well cured, might compete with that grown in any country.

Pine-Apples.—Little attention appears to be directed as yet to the cultivation of this finest West Indian fruit, although land of a very suitable character is found near most of the settlements. The soil should be a fine gravelly loam, free from clay and perfectly drained. The plants, consisting of suckers from older plants, may be put out at about $3\frac{1}{2}$ feet apart, care being taken to keep them free from weeds, and give the land, in dry weather, a dressing of decayed leaf-mould or rotten turf; animal manure, unless very old, and in fact reduced to black earth, is not suitable for pine-apples, and should be carefully avoided.

In rather moist lands, pines may be planted in ridges with drains between; but in hot dry soils, after a preparatory trenching of the whole surface, pines may be planted on level land.

The best kinds to cultivate for export are the Black Antigua, Black Jamaica or Cow-boy, Ripley, Charlotte Rothschild, Smooth Cayenne, Scarlet or Cuban Pine, and British Queen.

Cinchona.—At present, with the highlands, *i.e.*, above 3,000 feet, quite unexplored, it is doubtful whether cinchona can be placed amongst plants likely to succeed in British Honduras. On the occasion of my late visit, I was pointed out a tree at Government House supposed to be cinchona. This, however, was a plant of *Barringtonia speciosa*, a native of the East Indies.

It is possible that the Red Bark (*Cinchona succirubra*) may thrive on the higher slopes of the Cockscomb Mountains, but for the present, at least, with so many other valuable and more convenient industries, that of cinchona does not demand immediate attention.

Tea.—One kind of tea suitable for warm, steamy plains, viz., the Hybrid Assam, would thrive in many of the interior parts of the colony. The chief difficulty would be in fermenting, rolling, and firing the tea, so as to gain such prices in the market as would remunerate the planter.

An experienced planter from India or Ceylon, with a few coolies, would be able to start the industry, which, I doubt not, if it supplied only the local demands, and those of the neighbouring Republics, would prove commercially a success.

CHAPTER VII.

Nutmegs. Soil and situation. Rainfall. Curing of nutmegs and mace. Yield of trees. Pimento or Allspice. Cinnamon and camphor. Cardamoms. Elevation, soil, and shade. Returns per acre. Black pepper. Native peppers. Ipecacuanha: true and bastard. Variety from Carthagena. Ginger. Turmeric. Sarsaparilla. How cultivated in Jamaica. Returns per acre. Oil plants. Wanglo, pindar, castor-oil, palm-oil, and oil of Ben. Cloves. Fodder plants. Guinea grass. Para or water grass. Bahama grass. Natural grasses of the country. Rain-tree. Fodder and shade. Fruit-trees. Mango. Bread-fruit. Star-apple. Akee and Avocado pear. Mangosteen. Durian and new fruit-trees. Food plants. Yams, sweet potatoes, beans and cassava. Pumpkins, cucumbers, and melons. Vegetables and salads.

Nutmegs.—The cultivation of nutmegs is likely in every way to be successful in British Honduras, with its deep, rich alluvial soil on banks of rivers, and so admirably sheltered in most cases from strong winds.

The nutmeg-tree will not, however, thrive in a sandy soil, but prefers a deep, loamy, red, or friable soil; and while it requires a warm, humid atmosphere, and a plentiful supply of rain, it is very impatient of stagnant water near the roots. Again, "a spot selected for a nutmeg plantation cannot be too well sheltered, as high winds are most destructive to the tree, independently of the loss occasioned by the blowing off of fruit and flower." The nutmeg-trees may be planted in suitable districts, as indicated above, at about 25 feet to 30 feet apart; when first put out, the plants require to be well shaded, and if the weather be dry, to be watered regularly for a week or ten days.

It would not be advisable to establish nutmeg plantations in the hilly or mountainous portions of the colony, or in districts with a mean annual rainfall of less than 60 to 70 inches.

With regard to the preparation of the produce for the market, the nuts, after being thoroughly dried in the sun, cannot be too soon sent to the market. But with the mace (the aril of the nutmeg) it is otherwise. The latter must be kept until it has assumed a rich golden colour, which it does only after a lapse of several months. Red blades, that is, fresh mace, are looked upon with suspicion, and seriously affect the sale of the produce.

With regard to the yield from nutmeg-trees established under favourable circumstances, in Jamaica, trees at six years old give a return of about 1,500 to 2,000 nutmegs per annum. With trees say at 30 feet apart, and allowing one-third to be male or barren trees, this would give a return of 1,500 × 30 = 45,000 nutmegs per acre.

Taking an average of 90 nutmegs to the lb., the return in cash value would be 500 lbs. of nutmegs, at, say, 2s. per lb., equal to £50 per acre.

In the Botanic Gardens, Trinidad, the yield per tree, net, in the market has been over 20 lbs. (at 90 to the lb. this would be 1,800 nutmegs), with an average price of 2s. 2d. per lb. during the year. The value here per acre is at the rate of £60 per annum.

In both the above instances, it is only fair to mention that the calculations have been based on a comparatively small number of trees. The average yield over a large area, of say 40, 50, or 100 acres, would be correspondingly lower, but, even under any circumstances, it is evident that where suitable and favourable circumstances exist, as I believe they do in British Honduras, a nutmeg plantation is likely to be a very successful and remunerative undertaking.

Pimento.—Trees of this well-known spice plant, as already mentioned, are found in considerable numbers in the backwoods of the colony.

Whether it will prove advantageous to cultivate this spice in British Honduras remains to be seen. In Jamaica, the present system of establishing a pimento walk, is to allow a piece of land in the neighbourhood of pimento-trees to become overgrown with bush, which, in the course of time, is found to contain numerous pimento seedlings, grown from seeds devoured by birds and deposited there. When the plants are a certain size the bush is cleared, and the pimento-trees allowed to grow up.

With so many and so profitable objects, already at hand, I believe it is not advisable at present to take up this industry. It is strange that although pimento-trees grow in many other places besides Jamaica, the whole of the supply for the world's markets is obtained from this one island.

The demand for pimento, which is said to be used chiefly in the preparation of Russian leather, or, more probably, in the manufacture of liqueurs and cordials, would appear to be not increasing, and in some years the prices obtained are so low that they will not cover the cost of picking the crop.

Cinnamon and Camphor.—These plants, essentially East Indian, have not yet been cultivated in the West Indies on a commercial scale.

The tree yielding cinnamon (*Cinnamomum zeylanicum*) is thoroughly naturalised in Jamaica, where the bark is in general use amongst the peasantry, as a stomachic and a condiment.

It is not, however, exported, and it is doubtful whether it can be prepared by unskilled labour, so as to obtain remunerative prices.

The tree yielding camphor (*Cinnamomum camphora*) is fast growing, and likely to do well in British Honduras. It is already plentiful in many parts of the West Indies.

"The camphor of commerce is prepared from the wood by boiling the chopped branches in water, when after some time the camphor becomes deposited, and is purified by sublimation." The wood of the tree is sometimes used for making cabinets for the preservation of articles liable to injury by moths and insects.

Cardamoms.—For the higher lands, at elevations of 1,500 feet to 2,000 feet, this spice plant could be tried with every prospect of its cultivation being attended with success.

All that is necessary for this cultivation is, to underbush a suitable piece of forest, felling a tree here and there to let in a certain amount of air and light.

The cardamom plants, having much the habit of wild ginger, may then be put out at distances ranging from 6 to 8 feet apart. They require little cultivation beyond keeping the ground clear of rank-growing weeds. The flowers and fruit, the latter being small straw-coloured pods about half-an-inch long, are generally produced close to the ground, the widespreading panicles resting on the litter of fallen leaves and vegetable *débris*. The only preparation necessary with the crop is to collect the pods when ripe, and dry them in the sun, when they are ready for the market.

The return per acre from cardamoms is variously estimated at from 100 to 170 lbs. of cardamom pods, worth 3s. to 4s. per lb. Seeds of cardamoms can be obtained in quantities from Ceylon and Southern India (Malabar).

Black Pepper.—In many portions of the west and central districts, I came across vines of an indigenous pepper, closely resembling the ordinary black pepper of commerce. The aroma of the seeds, and indeed the general appearance of the plant, reminded me strongly of this valuable East Indian spice plant.

I have little doubt that the true black pepper could be grown in British Honduras in warm, moist situations, and with the necessary shade.

The plant is a climber, which easily attaches itself to rough-barked trees, of which many are common in the colony. The flowers—inconspicuous, and borne on long slender spikes—are followed by numerous reddish-black berries, which, when dried in the sun, become the familiar pepper-corns of commerce.

Ipecacuanha.—The true ipecacuanha of commerce is not a native of British Honduras, as commonly supposed. The plant passing under that name is the bastard ipecacuanha, or "Red Head" (*Asclepias curassavica*). Indian ipecacuanha is the produce of *Tylophora asthmatica*, a common plant throughout peninsular India, the island of Ceylon, and some parts of Mauritius.

The true ipecacuanha, is the produce of *Cephaëlis ipecacuanha*, a half-shrubby perennial, growing under shade of trees, in hot moist forests of Brazil.

A variety of this species has lately been found in Carthagena and New Granada, which is a larger and more robust plant than that from Brazil. This is now under trial in Jamaica, and it is probable that it will prove more amenable to cultivation than the Brazilian form, which, strange to say, has never been successfully treated on a large scale, even after some fifty years of experimental trial.

Ginger.—This plant (*Zingiber officinarum*) I noticed growing well in the neighbourhood of Mullin's River, but in rather indifferent soil. Perhaps no plant requires richer or finer soil than this spice, and there is no plant which exhausts it sooner and more thoroughly.

Its cultivation should be confined to the rich backwoods. I can hardly, however, recommend it on a large scale.

Turmeric.—This is a medicinal and tinctorial substance

obtained from the root of *Curcuma longa*, an East Indian plant belonging to the same family as the ginger. The powdered root forms one of the chief ingredients in the preparation of Indian curry-stuff, or curry-powder, to which it imparts its yellowish hue.

Plants of turmeric can easily be obtained from Jamaica, where it is completely naturalised in the warmer portions of the island.

Sarsaparilla.—Fine specimens of this valuable medicinal plant were met with wild, in the woods of the western districts, and I have no doubt that if systematically cultivated it would prove very remunerative.

It has much the habit of the common yam, and requires similar treatment.

In Jamaica, the plants, mostly seedlings, are put out at about 20 feet apart, and trained to stakes or trellises.

They begin to yield crop, consisting of the roots washed and dried in the sun, in about two or two-and-a-half years.

The first crop is said to yield as much as 20 lbs. of dried roots per plant; the second 30 to 40 lbs. per plant.

At the present price of sarsaparilla, the gross return is estimated at 30s. per plant, or per acre at about £50.

It may be mentioned that most of the sarsaparilla exported from British Honduras is obtained from the neighbouring Republics. There is, however, no reason, whatever, why a large trade may not be developed from sarsaparilla, partly collected from wild plants in the woods, as well as from plants under systematic cultivation. Plants are easily raised from seed, which is abundant during certain seasons in the woods.

Oil Plants.—Among the numerous class of oil plants for which the colony is adapted mention might be made of the wanglo (*Sesamum orientale*), which is already cultivated to a small extent among the settlers; pindar-nuts (*Arachis hypogæa*), a productive plant in light sandy soils; croton-oil-tree (*Croton tiglium*), a common East India plant; castor oil plant (*Ricinus communis*), already a common weed near cultivated areas; physic nut (*Jatropha curcas*), which yields a valuable medicinal oil; the African oil-palm (*Elæis guineensis*); the butter-tree (*Bassia butyracea*), a native of Bengal; and the horse-radish-tree, or oil of Ben tree (*Moringa pterygosperma*), a very free-growing and hardy tree, common in the West Indies.

Cloves.—This tree, yielding the cloves of commerce, has not, I believe, been tried in British Honduras, but it is very probable that it will grow well in free, well-drained soils and in sheltered situations, similar to those recommended for nutmegs. The portions of the tree which form an article of commerce are the dried calyces, or flower buds. After being gathered, these are prepared for shipment by smoking on hurdles covered with matting over a slow fire to give them a brown colour. The process is completed by further drying in the sun. The best kind of cloves are obtained from Penang, Bencoolen, Amboyna, and Zanzibar.

Fodder Plants.—At present, owing to the vast extent of uncleared forest land, fodder plants, such as good grasses, are not abundant in the colony. It is true that the vast stretches of land called "pine ridges" afford extensive pasture lands of rather coarse herbage for cattle and sheep, but for horses especially, it is very advisable to extend the cultivation of guinea grass (*Panicum jumentorum*), which appears to be admirably adapted to the colony. The water or Para grass (*Panicum barbinode*) has been introduced by some planters from Demerara, and for damp situations, quite beyond the reach of cultivated areas, it is an abundant and useful fodder plant. It is, however, very undesirable to introduce it anywhere where sugar-cane, bananas, coffee, corn, and cacao are likely to suffer from its prolific and wide-spreading habits.

When once it has established itself in canes or bananas, it is almost impossible to eradicate it, as the smallest joint will grow. Bahama grass (*Cynodon dactylon*) is already well established around Belize; it appears to thrive well in light, sandy soil. It does not, however, form an important fodder plant, at least in the localities indicated above.

The pastures, commons, or fields, in the neighbourhood of settlements, are easily formed after the forest is cut down by the natural grasses of the country.

Chief amongst these is *Paspalum distichum*, a wide-spreading, broad-leafed grass, which forms a close turf much liked by cattle. This grass is well adapted for permanent pastures, and if kept clean and not too severely grazed, it will yield a regular supply of valuable fodder.

So far as I could learn, little attention is paid in the colony to the cultivation of good fodder plants, and consequently extensive areas are devoted to the feeding of a few cattle, when under careful management one-third of the area would suffice.

It is a well-known axiom that to plant profitably, grazing (that is, the scientific treatment of grasses) should go hand in hand with sugar-cane growing, with bananas, oranges, and indeed with every tropical culture. For keeping horses and cattle in good condition on a small area, at the least possible expense; for supplying manure for gardens, nurseries, and fields, and, indeed, for the general work of the cultivator, nothing is likely to prove so profitable as a paddock of good rich-growing guinea grass, and clean, well-kept fields of the natural grasses of the country.

While on the subject of fodder plants, mention might be made of the Guango (*Pithecolobium saman*), a tree already established in the southern parts of the colony. This tree is a very desirable one near houses and outbuildings, as it both gives a grateful shade, and yields large quantities of pods, with a sweet pulp, which are greedily eaten by cattle.

For roadsides, cattle yards, and open spaces near sugar works, where shade is desired, no tree is more suitable or more profitable as a fodder plant than this.

Among the fruit-trees already in the colony, the Mango (*Mangifera indica*) is possibly the more widely distributed of any, especially at Belize and the settlements. The quality of the fruit is, however, not good; and many very valuable kinds might be introduced from Jamaica, Martinique, and Trinidad. In addition to supplying local demands, this luscious fruit might be exported to New Orleans, where there exists a large demand for it. It may be as well to mention, that grafted or layered plants of Mango are far preferable to seedlings: indeed it is only by grafting or layering that the choicest East Indian varieties can be propagated with certainty and success. The stocks for grafting may be seedlings from the ordinary mangoes of the country, which, for convenience of working and transit, may be established in bambu pots. Where mangoes do not bear, root-pruning is the best treatment.

The Bread-fruit, as in most West Indian colonies, is thoroughly established in British Honduras, where it affords a valuable and nutritious food. One very remarkable Bread-fruit-tree grows above the bridge in the town of Belize, equal to, if not finer than, anything seen in the West Indies. The best varieties of the Bread-fruit are propagated by root-suckers, as the fruits themselves are seedless. As a shade-tree for plantations the Bread-fruit is invaluable.

The Star-apple (*Chrysophyllum cainito*) does not appear to have been established here. This is a very highly-esteemed West

Indian fruit, which would, no doubt, thrive well in most of the river-side settlements.

The beautiful Akee (*Blighia sapida*), originally brought from the West Coast of Africa by slave ships, is now a common tree in the West Indies, and I noticed several fine specimens in Belize. The eatable portion of the fruit is the white spongy aril in which the jet-black seeds are partly immersed. This, when cooked, after carefully removing the stringy substance between the lobes, approaches the character of a custard, and is highly esteemed in most tropical countries. "Salt-fish and Akee" is a standing planter's dish in Jamaica.

The Avocado, or Alligator-pear (*Persea gratissima*), is a well-known vegetable, rather than a fruit, which might be extensively cultivated, both for home use as well as for exportation. There are two well-marked varieties—the green and the purple, the latter, from its larger size and finer flavour, being generally preferred in the West India Islands. The edible portion of the fruit is the firm pulp, enclosing the single large seed, which possesses a buttery or marrow-like taste, and hence called "subaltern's butter." The popular names of this fruit are supposed to have been derived from the Mexican term "ahuacatl"; the Spaniards corrupted this to "avocado," which means an advocate; and the English still further to "alligator-pear." A quantity of very superior oil, useful for illuminating and other purposes, may be obtained from the pulp by expression, samples of which were lately sent from Jamaica to the International Exhibition at Amsterdam.

The Loquat (*Eriobotrya japonica*) would find a congenial home on the rich lands at the western frontier; and, both on account of its prolific character as a fruit, as well as for the sake of its abundant foliage, used in many countries as food for cattle, it might be very well tried. The much-prized Mangosteen

(*Garcinia mangostana*), first in beauty and flavour amongst tropical fruits; the unique-flavoured Durian (*Durio zibethinus*), as well as the luscious Cherimoyer of Peru (*Anona cherimolia*), are also fruits which might be successfully introduced to the colony, and tend to improve the comfort and wealth of the inhabitants. In dry, well-drained situations to the south of Belize, the grape-vine (*Vitis vinifera*) is doing remarkably well, and its cultivation might be greatly extended. Among other fruits which might be cultivated are the Bhêl (*Ægle marmelos*), an East Indian fruit of an exquisite flavour and perfume, which is a specific in most tropical countries for dysentery and diarrhœa; the different varieties of Granadillas, Sweet-cups, Watermelons, &c., obtained from Passion flowers; the best qualities of Guavas; the Jew-plum (*Spondias dulcis*); the Para, or Brazil nut (*Bertholletia excelsa*); the Sabucaja nut (*Lecythis zabucajo*); the Ginep (*Melicocca bijuga*); the best varieties of Papaw (*Carica papaya*); the Tamarind (*Tamarindus officinalis*); the best cultivated varieties of the Naseberry (*Achras sapota*); the Wampee (*Cookia punctata*); the Date-palm (*Phœnix dactylifera*); the common Fig (*Ficus carica*); the Olive (*Olea eruropea*), and many other sub-tropical and tropical plants of economic value.

Of food plants proper, the chief, as already mentioned, is the Maize or Indian corn, which is raised in sufficient quantities for most local demands. On mahogany works, however, the workpeople's rations contain nothing raised in the country; but consist, chiefly, of American pork and flour, made into "doughboys" and "slap-jacks," both of which might, in a great measure, be replaced by native supplies of yams, sweet potatoes, cocos, pumpkins, bread-fruit, red and white peas (beans), cassava, gungo or pigeon-peas, &c. Of yams (*Dioscorea*) there are under cultivation, the negro yam, afou, white or buckra yam, and cassada yam. These require a warm, dry soil, on newly-cleared, rich forest land, and in such situations they yield in large quantities. The negroes of the West Indies live almost entirely on this nutritious esculent, and care for little else when they can get it. The sweet potato (*Batatas edulis*) will grow in all its varieties, abundantly, in British Honduras, and at all elevations, from sea-level to the highest lands of the interior. Cocos (*Colocasia esculenta*) might be utilised as shade-plants in young cacao plantations, and thus bring in a return sufficient to pay a portion of the working expenses. The same might be said of the cassava plant (*Manihot utilissima*), which, both as a vegetable and in the form of cassava bread, forms one of the staple foods of many races. The cassava plant is easily propagated by joints of the stem buried in the ground, and these, planted around a young cacao, Liberian coffee, nutmeg, or orange seedling, would give the shade so necessary to them in hot, dry districts, as well as a return in food-stuff, equal to about £5 to £8 per acre. What are called the red and white peas—really varieties of haricot beans—are freely grown in tropical countries, and form a most nutritious and valuable food. None of these plants are cultivated in British Honduras to the extent they deserve; but I am hopeful that when planters have carefully considered the wonderful advantages they possess, and have become fully convinced of the numberless resources within their reach, they will not be slow to take advantage of them.

All kinds of pumpkins, cucumbers, marrows, and melons should grow on the rich, well-drained soils of the interior; care being taken to plant all these, as much as possible, in freshly-broken land, to avoid the numerous diseases to which they are liable. A member of this family, the chiote or chocho (*Sechium edule*), might be introduced from Jamaica, where it is a hardy, self-sown climber, bearing nearly all the year round a fruit larger than a pear, covered with soft prickles. It is boiled (or parboiled and fried) and eaten as a vegetable, and resembles a vegetable marrow. Tomatoes, for which there is a great demand in the States, might be grown to any extent, and if shipped during the winter months they would command very remunerative prices.

Of ordinary vegetables, such as cabbages, peas, beans, parsnip, carrots, beet, artichoke, and onions; and of salads, such as lettuce, radish, chillies, eschalots, and endive, every garden around a planter's house might produce supplies, equal to those of any tropical country. I was much struck, during my visit, by the entire absence in the colony of any attempt to keep up a vegetable garden, or indeed to raise many plants of everyday use, even in the neighbourhood of the best houses. With the introduction of new plants, and it is hoped with the more widely-recognised feeling that the land is capable of being rendered amenable to culture and productive at a very small outlay, this neglect will give place to greater activity, and to a desire to make the country, not merely a passing sojourning place, while engaged in amassing wealth, but a home, surrounded by all the appliances and comforts of civilised life.

CHAPTER VIII.

Labour question. Indigenous labour: how to improve. Masters and Servants Act. Carib. Indian. Cooly immigration. Views of Sir Frederick Barlee. Advance and Truck systems. Local enterprise. Crown lands. Conditions of sale. Navigable rivers. Steam communication with New Orleans, New York, and London. Railways. Agricultural Board. Botanic Gardens. Importation and distribution of seeds and plants. Geological Survey. Climate of British Honduras. Meteorological observations. Price of food. House-rent. Horses. Currency. Religion. Education. Hints to intending settlers.

ONE of the first questions, which the pioneer and planter has to deal with in a new country, is that of labour. In British Honduras, with a small indigenous or native population, the great bulk of the labourers required to develop the country must necessarily be attracted from outside.

Before, however, discussing the circumstances attending the importation of labour it might be advantageous to consider the present labour resources of the colony, and in what respects they are capable of being utilised and improved.

The Belize Creoles, of African descent, but with an admixture of Spanish and Indian blood, are a strong, powerful race, admirably suited to the heavy labour of mahogany cutting, which, indeed, they prefer to that of ordinary tillage. They are characterised by a random recklessness as regards the future, with, however, a keen sense of keeping up the regular Christmas orgies in Belize, when their engagement in the bush has expired. The Creole labour is probably only sufficient to maintain the mahogany and logwood cutting industries of the country in their present position; but during the times of depression, when the market value of mahogany and logwood is low, a large proportion of the indigenous Creole labour is thrown out of employ, and at such times, it is available for felling forest and clearing land, operations for which it is specially adapted.

The so-called Spaniards of the colony, consisting chiefly of Ladinos and Mestizos, are, as the names indicate, a mixed race, partly Spanish and partly Indian.

They form an increasing portion of the population, and come to British Honduras from the neighbouring Republics to the west and south, viz., Guatemala, Spanish Honduras, and Mosquito Coast, or from Yucatan in the north. Those from the latter country are generally small in stature and light coloured; whereas those from the south are dark coloured and generally finer men. It is probable that many of these men, especially from the south, are fugitives from justice, and only remain in the colony long enough to allow of their safe return when political and other troubles have passed away.

There are several Carib settlements in the colony, which furnish a fine race of men and women capable of turning their hands almost to anything. The men are admirable sailors, and they are of essential service in navigating the numerous waterways of the country and in carrying produce to Belize.

The Carib women principally supply the local markets with yams and starch.

The Caribs are naturally timid and shy, and, as mentioned by Mr. Fowler, "their ambition is to be left alone, and live as their forefathers have lived before them; if disturbed or annoyed they simply move to another place."

Although a number of Caribs work occasionally with Creoles on mahogany works, it is doubtful whether any appreciable labouring population can be recruited from this source.

Of pure Indians there are some small settlements in the

colony, as at San Francisco, near Orange Walk, Old River, and in the north; but most of those engaged as labourers on sugar estates are Spanish Indians. Of these the Waikas, from the Mosquito Coast, form an important element. They are small, wiry men, unsuited to the heavy labour of mahogany-cutting, but of quiet, plodding habits, which, combined with the lower wages demanded, render them an important element in the labour market. There is no doubt that if a fair and encouraging system of immigration were organised with the Mosquito Coast, and especially, if the passages of labourers to and fro were guaranteed, the Waikas would come to Belize in much larger numbers.

Of labourers indigenous to the colony or introduced from the immediate neighbourhood, there would appear, according to the above remarks, to be four classes, viz., the Belize Creole, the Spaniard, the Carib, and the Indian. Of these, possibly, the latter is the only class capable of being considerably increased.

Of labourers imported from other parts, but chiefly from the British West India Islands, there are two classes, viz., the West Indian Creole (negro), and time-expired Coolies. The greater number, if not, indeed, the whole of the individuals composing these two classes, are introduced by private means from Jamaica and Barbados, attracted no doubt by the offer of free passages and higher rates of wages.

Both the Creoles and the Coolies are well adapted for field work, and they easily fall into the ways of the country.

According to the census of 1881, there were resident in the colony 834 persons (probably all labourers) returned as natives of Jamaica; this shows an increase of 408 on the number returned in the census for 1871.

Of natives of Barbados, the number returned for 1881 was 204, which, compared with 230 returned in 1871, shows a slight decrease in the number of persons of Barbadian birth still resident in the colony.

The Coolies, working chiefly on the sugar estates, are for the most part time-expired Coolies from Jamaica, who, having been originally introduced by the Immigration Department of that island, are at liberty, at the end of five years, to return to India or to remain in the West Indies as labourers on their own terms. Of such Coolies at present in British Honduras, there are about 200 engaged on sugar estates and small plantations; and as the colony has a good name amongst this class of labourers it is probable the number will increase.

Captain Marriner, who has very obligingly given me a memorandum on the labour question in British Honduras, remarks :—". . . The rate of wages in this colony is high in comparison with other parts of the West Indies, but it varies very much in different districts. The Creole, the Spaniard, and the Carib get from $7 to $12 a month, in addition to rations, or $15 to $18 a month without rations. The rations consist of 4 lbs. salt pork and 7 quarts of flour a week.

"The Indian and Cooly will work for $11 a month and find himself, or $4 a month with rations.

"In all cases tools and implements are found by the employer.

"There is a special Act of Legislature, called 'The Master and Servants Act,' peculiar to the colony, under which all labourers hire. Many of its conditions are considered hard and severe upon the servant; but it is also binding on the master. Most of the labourers know what they have a right to, and they get it.

"There is another matter, peculiar, I believe, to this colony, and that is the advance system.

"Under the 'Master and Servants Act,' above mentioned, a labourer cannot be hired for more than twelve months. The hiring season is about the end of the year, December, and it is carried out almost entirely in Belize, the chief town of the colony, so that both employer and employed flock to Belize in large numbers towards this time. The labourer wants money to buy clothes, and a few articles necessary for him to take with him to his new engagement in the bush, as well as a little spare cash to enable him to enjoy his brief holiday in town. The employer makes the agreement between himself and his servant more binding on the latter, by getting him at once into debt to his master; this is done by giving the servant, on his hiring, from two to six months' wages in advance; much, if not all, of which is spent in the various stores and grog shops of the town.

"The Carib and the Creole do well for mahogany works, and sometimes the Spaniard, but they, and certainly the Indian, with the Cooly, are best suited for the lighter work in the field; and if there is to be more agriculture in this country, there must be more labour, and if it can be procured at a cheaper rate than now prevails, so much the better. . . ."

There is no doubt that for a regular and satisfactory supply of labour, the colony must ultimately depend upon arrangements being made, with the Government of India, for the importation of Coolies, on the same terms as they are now supplied to Demerara, Trinidad, Grenada, and Jamaica. This would put an end at once to the labour difficulty, and afford a reasonable guarantee that there would be no loss to capitalists under any circumstances, that might arise, with regard to the demands for mahogany and logwood cutting.

Coolies might be obtained from India at the rate of, say, £15 per head, of which the repayment would be spread over the five years during which their engagement lasts. During this time the wages would be fixed at the rate of 1s. per day, all things included. For light field work in the tropics, the Cooly is an invaluable worker. Demerara, Trinidad, and Grenada, without Coolies, would never have attained their present prosperous condition.

And what has been done in these colonies, with Coolies, may likewise be done in British Honduras, which, from the richness of its natural resources, would eventually become one of the most prosperous British possessions in this part of the world.

Sir Frederick P. Barlee, speaking at a late meeting of the Royal Colonial Institute, was, however, of opinion that Cooly labour was not actually required, at present, in developing the resources of the colony, and expressed an opinion that "there is no real difficulty in British Honduras procuring such labour as it requires. I am sure," he said, "there would be small difficulty in getting labour from the United States, where the price of labour is not much in excess of that in the colony. Again, at St. Thomas and the islands adjacent to it, there is an ample supply of labour available, and at the Bahamas there is also a large number of the labouring population unable to procure remunerative labour, who would be glad to find their way to British Honduras on reasonable terms. I am glad to have the opportunity of stating these things, for they are facts; and I am sure that people who will take the trouble to invest their money in the colony will find themselves repaid over and over again."

The advance system, to which reference has been made above by Captain Marriner, is evidently most objectionable, and pernicious in its tendencies, and doubtless in time it will be abolished: It has arisen and gradually grown from the peculiar circumstances incidental to the solitary and remote life of most of the mahogany-cutters, who, having only one holiday in the year, are determined to "keep Christmas" in accordance with the old customs of the settlement. If all employers were to combine, and if all hired on the same plan, and resolutely set their faces against the advance system, it might be abolished within a very short period. There is no doubt that the system places the labourer more completely in the power of the employer, and it may have had its uses amidst the lawlessness of former days; but there can be no justification of its use at present, and its continuance as an institution connected with the employment of labour in the colony is to be greatly deplored. Associated with the advance system, and indeed an integral part of it, is the so-called truck system, which requires, or at least encourages, the labourers to take a portion of their wages in goods from their employer's store. When in the remote woods of the interior, with no stores within some thirty or forty miles, the employer must naturally supply the labourers with necessary food and tools; but under every circumstance, and especially in the neighbourhood of settlements, it would be far better to pay the workmen in cash once a fortnight or once a month; and allow them to make their purchases wherever they please. The flocking to Belize at Christmas-time of nearly every one connected with the mahogany works, tends to foster the spirit of dissipation and recklessness which characterises the mahogany and logwood cutter; but unless hiring-places are established at different places in the colony, and recognised by a mutual arrangement between the employer and employed, it is difficult to break through an old-established custom; and the more so, that to many it is an absolute necessity to visit Belize, at least once or twice a year. For the most part, I believe, employers in the colony treat their workpeople fairly and honestly; and it is with no desire to reflect upon them that exception is taken to systems which they did not create, but which, nevertheless, are quite inconsistent with the spirit of liberty and personal freedom, to which they, no less than their workpeople, lay claim as the birthright of Englishmen.

As indicating that the residents in the colony have strong faith in its capabilities and prospects, and are prepared to invest their savings in it, four small companies have been organised for the acquisition of land, and the cultivation of fruit for the American market. As mentioned in the account of my visit to that locality, two of these companies are established on the Mullin's River, namely, the British Honduras Fruit Company, with a capital of $5,000; and the Belize Fruit Company, also with a capital of $5,000. The larger Walize Fruit Company, with a capital of $15,000, is on the Monkey River; while the Manatee Fruit Company is established on Soldier Creek. With careful management and favourable seasons these undertakings have every prospect of success; and, as already they have large areas under cultivation in bananas, the returns with this early maturing and prolific crop should yield handsome returns on the capital invested. I regard these local efforts as most favourable indications of the energy and spirit of enterprise which characterise the people of British Honduras, and as also of the strong faith which they have in the land of their adoption.

The extent of land in possession of the Crown is very large in the south, where the chief unopened forest-lands lie. In the north the Crown has hardly any land. The Crown lands lie south of a line drawn from the Sibun River to Garbutt's Falls; and, with the exception of a few lots on lease or already sold, include the rich lands on Indian Creek (Sibun River), Manattee River, Mullin's River, the upper lands on the North Stann Creek and Sittee River, embracing the Cockscomb country, as well as a large extent of back-lands in the interior on the frontier, as far as the river Temash. Naturally the coast lands, and those within easy reach of the rivers, are being taken up first; but, including all Crown and private lands, there are probably over a million acres of fine cohune-ridge, or alluvial virgin soil, in

British Honduras, of which, according to a late return, only some ten thousand acres, or less than one-hundredth part, is, or has been, under cultivation. The Crown lands are offered at "not less than one dollar an acre;" and private lands are no doubt also available at moderate rates.

Under an Ordinance, No. 8 of 1879, Crown lands in British Honduras may be obtained from Government under the following conditions:—

"Town lands shall be offered by public auction at an upset price to be recommended by the Surveyor-General of Crown Lands, and approved by the Lieutenant-Governor in Council, and may be put up either by order of the Lieutenant-Governor, or upon the application of some person who shall at the time of making such application deposit 10 per cent. of the upset price. Such deposits shall, if no advance on the upset price be made, be considered as part payment on completion of purchase; an amount equal to 10 per cent. on the purchase-money shall be paid on the fall of the hammer when lands are put up for sale by order of the Lieutenant-Governor. In every case the balance shall be paid within thirty days from the day of sale, and in default thereof the purchaser shall forfeit his purchase-money and also all right of title to the land.

"Rural or country lands shall be sold without auction at not less than one dollar an acre; and the minimum acreage of rural sections shall be five acres, but any land so shut in by private lands or other bounds as not to contain five acres, may be sold at such rate as the Lieutenant-Governor, on the recommendation of the Surveyor-General of Crown Lands, may direct.

"It shall be lawful for the Lieutenant-Governor to issue licenses for five years to persons desirous to occupy waste lands of the Crown, in sections not less than fifty nor more than five hundred acres, for purposes of cultivation or improvement, at a yearly rent of 10 cents an acre, with right to purchase at any time during the tenancy, or such licenses may be renewed by the Lieutenant-Governor.

"A location ticket will be issued to persons authorised to occupy any portion of Crown Lands, which will be exchanged for a grant on the block of land being surveyed. No costs of survey will be charged, but a uniform fee of five dollars will be charged for every deed of grant, and a fee of one dollar for recording the same.

"Application to purchase or lease should be made to the Surveyor-General of Crown Lands, or at the offices of the paid magistrates in the rural districts, at whose offices forms of application can be had; and a deposit of one dollar is required to accompany an application to purchase, and two dollars and a half on an application to lease.

"Persons already occupying Crown Lands may obtain grants or leases of the same upon such terms as may appear to the Lieutenant-Governor just and reasonable, provided His Excellency shall see fit to grant the same after taking all the circumstances into his consideration."

The chief carrying work of the colony is effected by water by means of dug-outs, called, according to their shape, pit-pans, dorays, and bungays; the former are restricted to the rivers, while the two latter are much used along the coast. As indicating the excellent river system and means of transit afforded by the natural water-ways of the colony, I quote the following table from the Honduras Almanack (Wilson), 1880:—

NAVIGABLE DISTANCE UP RIVERS.

River				Miles
Hondu	navigable from its bar towards source,			60 miles.
New River	,,	,,	,,	60 ,,
Old River	,,	,,	,,	120 ,,
Sibun	,,	,,	,,	30 ,,
Manattee	,,	,,	,,	16 ,,
Mullin's	,,	,,	,,	16 ,,
Sittee	,,	,,	,,	16 ,,
North Stann Creek	,,	,,	,,	18 ,,
Sarstoon	,,	,,	,,	10 ,,

The rivers smaller than these are all navigable, for a few miles from the bar.

Steam communication by Royal Mail steamers, which connect Belize and New Orleans, by a fortnightly service, has proved a wonderful stimulus to fruit culture. The contractor is bound to give preference in the purchase of fruits and other products to those grown within the colony, provided the prices and quality are equal to what might be obtainable outside the colony.

The mail communication between Europe and British Honduras is carried on, *via* New York, by the Atlantic steamers, from Liverpool; thence by train to New Orleans, where the mail steamer for Belize is authorised to await the arrival of the English mails.* British Honduras is included in the Postal Union, and the usual rates of postage are in force. Locally, the postage is twopence and one penny, according to distance. Newspapers, of which there are two (*The Belize Advertiser* and *Colonial Guardian*), are carried locally free of postage. From London to Belize, *via* New York and New Orleans, the mails generally take eighteen to twenty days; passengers might also accomplish the journey within the same time. Through tickets are issued from New York to Belize per rail and contract steamer, including sleeping car, for £19; this, with £18 for the passage from Liverpool to New York, will make the total journey from England to Belize cost about £37.

Direct communication between London and Belize (calling at Nassau and Jamaica) is effected about once a month by the London line of steamers (Messrs. Scrutton, Sons & Co., 9, Gracechurch Street, London). The cabin passage is about £25; and rates of freight from 35s. to 70s. per ton.

Between Belize and Philadelphia, Warner & Merritt's line of steamers sail once a month, calling also at Livingstone, Honduras, and the Bay Islands. Communication by independent steamers and sailing vessels is being organised between British Honduras and many ports in other parts of the States, and

---

* Particulars of this service may be obtained from P. Leckie & Co., 34, Lime Street, London; Macheca Bros., 129, Decatin Street, New Orleans; and P. Leckie & Co., Agents, Belize.

especially in the interest of the fruit trade. At present the shipping facilities are ample for the requirements of the colony; and the demand for fruit is greater than the supply.

Telegraphic communication, by means of La Compagnie du Télégraphe Sous Marine de L'Amérique Centrale, is in course of being effected, which will land cables and construct telegraphs in or through the colony, connecting it with the island of Cuba. The colony has guaranteed a payment of £1,000 annually for twenty years, as the proceeds of telegraphic despatches sent from and received in the colony, so long as the cable is in working order.

Until the direct cable is established, telegrams to Belize, and British Honduras generally, should be sent to New Orleans, to be forwarded by the next contract mail steamer to Belize.

The water-ways of British Honduras, though so extensive and so largely utilised, require to be largely supplemented before the rich virgin lands on the upper portions of the Sibun and Belize Rivers can be adequately worked. Not only this, but the natural supplies of valuable woods which first attracted notice, are becoming partially exhausted in the immediate neighbourhood of the rivers, and they can only be brought down to the coast by means of railways. Hence the question of a railway, which in the first instance is intended to run through the valley of the Old or Belize River, is being warmly taken up in the colony, and its construction is expected to give a great incentive to agriculture, as well as open up new fields for the older staples. From a recent notice in *The Colonies and India* I find that—

"The general idea is to construct a railway from Belize westward to the Guatemala frontier, and thence through Peten, Coban, &c., to the capital, Guatemala City, where, besides the area within the colony, it will open up immense commercial, agricultural, and mineral fields.

"So far as the colony itself is concerned, the proposal is to build a railway from the town of Belize, running south of the Belize or Old River, through Crown lands, to the boundary of Guatemala, in the direction of Garbutt's Falls, thus opening up virgin forests, abounding in all the precious woods, &c., already mentioned, the produce of which can be brought to market only by means of a railway. The revenue derivable from this trade would be very large.

"A grant of land three miles on either side of the line is intended to be given to the constructors of the railway, embracing a total area of 384,000 acres. Of these lands it is proposed that the railway shall give free grants to actual settlers of alternate blocks of as much as they can bring under cultivation, reserving the other alternate blocks for sale in open market.

"The estimated length of the line is 100 miles. The gauge will be 3 feet, and the proposed capital of the company will be £500,000, in 5,000 shares of £100 each. The proposal has been generally approved by the Colonial Government, and has, we believe, been submitted to the favourable consideration of the Secretary of State for the Colonies."

One of the chief wants of the country, next to the solution of the labour question, is to obtain due supplies of seeds and plants for establishing large areas under cultivation. Of bananas, plantains, and coco-nuts, there is an abundant supply of "suckers" and seeds always available in the colony. The valuable rubber-tree, cacao, vanilla, sarsaparilla, and many other plants, are found wild in the woods, and but little care and attention is needed to procure seeds or plants. But for nutmeg, cloves, tea, cardamoms, best kinds of oranges, limes, lemons, fine seed of tobacco, plants of cinnamon, camphor, black pepper, ipecacuanha, ginger, turmeric, oil plants, fodder plants, and the numerous choice and valuable fruit-trees which I have suggested for the colony, there should be a well-organised system adopted, either by means of an Agricultural Board or Botanic Garden, which should give special attention to their introduction and distribution. I believe an Agricultural Board was intended to be formed in 1879, in accordance with the report of a Select Committee of the Legislative Council.

This Committee felt that with such a fertile soil available on easy terms, energy and industry on the part of the inhabitants are all that are now requisite to grow fruit in large quantities, with every prospect of profitable returns.

At the same time the Committee were sensible of exceptional circumstances which had militated against the cultivation of the soil from the earliest history of the colony; and recognised the desirableness of some steps being taken to assist cultivators in the absence of experience and knowledge of the subject on their part.

To carry this out in a practical and satisfactory way the Committee suggested the formation of an Agricultural Board, with an annual grant. The duties of such a Board were to be to procure all necessary information relating to products adapted to the soil and climate, and suitable for available markets, and disseminate such information gratuitously and as widely as possible.

Simple directions for the cultivation of the several products might also be printed separately or in small pamphlet form and distributed freely. Seeds and plants might be procured, through the instrumentality of this Board, with a view to obtaining the best species or introducing new products into the colony.

Although this report was adopted, and an Agricultural Board appointed, it does not appear that any practical results followed.

It is much to be desired that this Board, with a small annual grant, should be revived, and that it be connected with a government department, and submit an annual report on its operations. Such a Board would require a *depôt* either at Belize or at one of the southern settlements, where some plants, especially those of a delicate nature, might be raised from seed, and where others not capable of immediate distribution might be stored. Where the distribution by seed is practicable, it should always be adopted; but as most of the valuable objects enumerated above are obtainable only as plants, there must of necessity be a small garden, with sheds and beds, properly laid out, to receive these plants, and to take care of them until fit for removal.

With regard to the dissemination of general knowledge respecting the cultivation of economic plants, this might be very effectively done by means of clearly-worded pamphlets and circulars, supplemented by short notices in the *Official Gazette*, and in the local Almanack.*

There are, at present, numerous works and periodicals devoted to the interests of tropical agriculture, which should find a place on the table of every planter, as well as be included in any public library that may exist in the colony. A list of useful books for planters is given in the Appendix.

I have already suggested that, as soon as possible, a small Botanic Garden should be established, which, for its cost and utility, will be found, after all, the most economical, as well as the most effective means of carrying on the work sketched out for the Agricultural Board. Such a garden would soon become an institution of great importance and utility, and, as in most colonies, prove most acceptable to the people.

If the railway were formed, connecting Belize with the rich back-lands on the Old River, the garden might be established some few miles out of Belize, so as to afford facilities for

---

* One of the best and most comprehensive of current periodicals is the *Tropical Agriculturist*, published by Messrs. A. M. & J. Ferguson, at the *Observer* Press, Ceylon (A. & J. Haddon, Bouverie Street, London). This contains original articles and letters bearing upon most tropical plants; as, also, a large summary of valuable information connected with the industrial application of plant products. Other periodicals, such as the *Planter's Gazette, Gardener's Chronicle, Colonies and India*, &c., treat on colonial economic plants, and often afford valuable hints to planters.

shipping plants from Belize to the southern settlements, as well as supply the demands of planters on the Old River. Being near to Belize, and in close communication with the headquarters of the Government, the institution might be more easily supervised. It would also be conveniently at hand to receive plants on arrival from other countries, and place them under immediate treatment.

In the absence of railway facilities at Belize, the Botanic Garden might be established at Mullin's River, and only a few miles inland, where there would be good facilities for receiving and shipping plants.

A Botanic Garden, by showing practically the best methods for the treatment and propagation of plants, by training natives and others in the art of gardening, and in the management of nurseries, in diffusing information respecting the treatment of the diseases of plants, as also in saving large sums too often wasted in new countries in worthless experiments, would prove most valuable. All that would be required at first would be a small plot of ground for experimental cultivation, and a nursery; the establishment might grow as the resources of the colony are more fully developed, until at last it might become a recognised institution, contributing largely to the wealth of the colony, and fostering every effort to promote its welfare and prosperity. The initial expenses of a small garden such as I recommend would be about £500 per annum, including the superintendent or manager's salary, and the necessary labour.

Until a trained gardener arrives in the colony, it would be well to continue to make collections of all its indigenous plants and have them carefully examined and described. I trust that my recommendations, under this head, which have been already submitted to the Government, will be adopted. There are doubtless numerous valuable plants still to be found in the woods of the interior, and these only await the systematic efforts of the collector, and the determinations of science, to render them available for the general welfare of the country.

Another important step which might tend to develop the resources of the colony is a careful survey of its chief geological features. As to what the scope of such survey should be, reference may be made to the Memoirs of the West India Geological Survey, already completed for Jamaica, Trinidad, and British Guiana. In addition to testing for minerals and ores, and in critically examining the nature and characteristics of the rocks, a geological survey would bring scientific knowledge and research to bear upon the chief economic resources of the soil, and point out their chemical constituents. In fact, a geological survey of the colony is now one of its chief wants, and provided its finances can bear the expense (which, however, might be spread over several years), the results, apart from finding gold and silver, cannot fail to prove most valuable and suggestive.

I brought with me numerous samples of soils from British Honduras, with the intention of having them analysed; but the permission to incur the expenses did not reach me in time to include the results in this work. The general characters of the soils, however, were of a most promising character.

The climate of the colony, as well as that of Belize, has been already incidentally discussed in course of the previous pages.

The general conclusions arrived at will, I believe, point to the fact that, either through ignorance or prejudice, the climate of British Honduras, taking the colony as a whole, has been greatly maligned.

That the legislature of British Honduras has a firm belief in the healthiness of the colony is shown by the fact that a local ordinance, referring to the registration of medical practitioners, has a preamble somewhat as follows:—" Whereas, owing to the salubriousness of the climate of British Honduras, there are few inducements for medical men to settle therein, it is hereby enacted," &c., &c.

Quoting from the Honduras Almanack (1882), the characteristic features of the climate of British Honduras during the greater part of the year are a most equable temperature, with strong easterly breezes in the summer months or dry season, an absence of rain for three or four months from the end of January, and in the winter months cold northerly winds, which are generally dry and bracing, and land winds, fortunately not continuous, which usually bring a good deal of moisture from the neighbouring collections of water, and much rain. Exposed to the full influence of the trade-winds, the whole coast may be considered as unexceptionally healthy during their continuance, while the temperature does not vary more than six or eight degrees during the twenty-four hours. The atmosphere is dry: indeed it would be difficult to point out any place in the West Indies in which the humidity is so inconsiderable. The dew which falls at night is almost imperceptible, and it is only where the country is high and in close proximity to hills, that the dews may be considered noticeable. During the rainy season, the commencement of which is variable, there are sometimes short periods of calm, in which, although the temperature is not appreciably heightened, the feeling of heat is great, but fortunately these calms are of rare occurrence and short duration. The rainfall is variable, but from observations extending over a period of eighteen years, the general average for a year is found to be between 75 and 80 inches.

Europeans form but a small part of the population of British Honduras, but sickness of every kind prevails to a much smaller extent among them than in the black population. The principal diseases affecting them are intermittent and remittent fevers and liver affections, and these are generally of the mildest description. The climate is such that a healthy European will undergo as much fatigue and exposure without being affected by it as he would in his own country; and where ordinary care is taken, a moderately good constitution may resist the effects of climate for a long period of years without experiencing even the smallest degree of sickness. The mortality among them is small, and, apart from special causes, they can show a degree of healthiness equalling, if not surpassing, that of their own country. Some years ago, white troops were regularly stationed here, and although the sanitary arrangements for soldiers in those days were very different from what they are now, they enjoyed good health, and perhaps they were never stationed anywhere in any of the colonies, more particularly in the West Indies, where the sickness and mortality among them were so little. In the beginning of 1867, when the troublesome raids of the Indians on our frontier took place, the detachment of white artillery which accompanied the expedition against them underwent, equally with the black troops, the fatigues of long marches through dense bush and virgin forests, with probably less discomfort, and certainly with much less sickness afterwards, than was complained of by the black soldiers.

The diseases which affect the coloured population are similar to some of those affecting the blacks of other colonies in the West Indies, but there is an absence of many of the most serious, as typhus and typhoid fevers, small-pox, scrofula and leprosy. Epidemics are very unfrequent, and are not of that terrible, sweeping nature which characterises epidemics in the West Indies generally. Within the memory of the oldest inhabitant small-pox has only prevailed once, viz., in the year 1856; and in the years 1860 and 1869 there were a few sporadic cases of yellow fever, confined principally to the white population. For men who have already had experience in tropical countries, there is nothing in the climate of British Honduras which they have to fear. The fact already alluded to, namely, of the existence of a settlement of white emigrants from the Southern States who have established comfortable homes at almost sea-level, and turned, by their own hands, a wild tropical forest into a number of rich and prosperous plantations, sufficiently indicates the general healthiness of the country. Writing of this settlement in 1878, Lieutenant-Governor Barlee remarks, that although some five or six families have lived here for a period of nine years, *not a single death has occurred among them, nor any illness other than of a temporary nat re.*

From a very careful series of returns prepared by the medical officer of health (Dr. Hunter), and his colleague (Dr. Muir), the following table has been compiled.

MEAN READINGS OF METEOROLOGICAL OBSERVATIONS AT BELIZE FOR THE PAST FOUR YEARS.

Year.	Reading of Barometer, Means of				Thermometer, Means of						Rainfall.	
	Year.	Highest.	Lowest.	Range.	Highest.	Lowest.	Range.	Of all highest.	Of all lowest.	Range.	No. of Days.	Quantity Collected.
1878	29·92	30·35	29·75	0·60	88·22	71·37	16·85	84·92	76·56	8·36	146	105·49
1879	30·04	30·38	29·80	0·58	89·50	60·00	29·50	83·25	74·00	9·25	174	91·24
1880	30·03	30·32	29·70	0·62	90·50	61·00	29·50	83·50	71·50	12·00	126	77·74
1881	29·89	30·02	29·75	0·27	90·50	62·00	28·50	83·65	74·07	9·58	147	91·46

The annual mean temperature at sea-level is 79·5° Fah.; in the interior it is considerably lower. For instance, at Orange Walk (Old River) in November last, at 6 a.m., the thermometer often stood at 67° Fah.; and sometimes, especially during the prevalence of cold northerly winds, I have no doubt it would fall much lower.

As regards the prices of the ordinary articles of consumption, bread and rice sell at 3d. per pound; beef, rather tough, 6d. to 9d. per pound; pork, with a good supply, 6d. to 9d. per pound; mutton, rather scarce, 1s. per pound; turtle, plentiful, 6d. per pound; fish, abundant and good, about 1d. per pound; fowls, poor, 2s. each; turkeys, cheap and good, 3s. each; ducks, scarce, 2s. each. General retail shopping, either in dry goods or preserved provisions, can be done in Belize on a slight advance of prices in England and the States; in many cases articles can be bought in Belize of better quality and cheaper than in the West India Islands; while the large and well-built stores " are exceptionally well furnished with all kinds of goods."

House-rent, in Belize and the larger settlements, ranges from 25s. to £6 per month, according to position and accommodation.

Horses, chiefly raised from Spanish breeds, are moderately cheap; a good strong pony, admirably suited for threading the bush-tracks and mahogany-truck paths of the country, and crossing creeks, may be had for £25. Bullocks and mules are chiefly used for draught purposes, horses being reserved for lighter work and riding.

It would appear that all the money of the neighbouring Republics is current in Belize: for Mexican, Guatemalan, and American dollars pass, side by side, with English shillings and half-crowns. Gold is seldom seen. As there is no Bank in the colony, great inconvenience is often felt in keeping and disbursing large sums; as, in the absence of gold and paper money, they usually consist of a wonderful assortment of silver coin.

The principal and official language of the colony is English. The negroes speak Creole-English, so well known in the West India Islands; the other elements speak Spanish, which is not Castilian; Maya, the chief language of the Indians; and Carib.

As regards religion, there is no established Church; the

clergy being for the most part supported by their respective congregations. The Church of England is included in the diocese of Jamaica. The majority of the people, arising no doubt from the Spanish element, were returned in the census of 1871 as Roman Catholics. The numbers being: Roman Catholics, 15,000, Protestants 9,000. In the latter were included members of the Wesleyan and Baptist congregations, as well as the Church of England.

The schools in the colony are generally connected with the religious denominations, and superintended by the clergy. By a late return, two schools are Church of England, ten Roman Catholic, ten Wesleyan, and one Baptist. The teachers are granted certificates according to merit, and receive a certain amount of Government aid.

Before closing this chapter, it may be well to mention, that the men most likely to succeed in a new country like British Honduras are those which have already had some experience in a tropical country, and are able to bring some capital with them. As I mentioned lately in a paper read before the Royal Colonial Institute—

"For the last thirty or forty years, the tide of emigration, as regards tropical planters, and consequently the flow of capital, has steadily set to the eastward, and thousands of men possessing means and energy have settled on the Nilgiris, on the slopes of the Himalayas, and on the mountains of Ceylon, to cultivate tea, coffee, and cinchona. More recently they have gone still further east, to Perak, Johore, Sumatra, and Borneo.

"Now, however, that the dreadful coffee-leaf disease has induced so depressing an influence in all Eastern countries; and whilst Englishmen are contemplating investing their capital in countries not under British rule, and in places so remote and so little accessible to the chief markets of the world, it seems not inappropriate to consider what lands, what facilities for culture, and what returns on capital, the West Indies—within some eighteen days of England, and in close and easy communication with the vast markets of Europe and America—have to offer the pioneer and the planter."

I have no hesitation whatever in stating, from my knowledge of the East Indies, that British Honduras, in the surpassing richness of its soil, in its wonderful facilities for the growth of numerous tropical plants, and in its proximity to, and close connection with, the large and increasing markets of the United States and Canada, possesses advantages unequalled in any country in the East Indies; and, especially in those, such as Perak, Johore, and Borneo, where all the difficulties and drawbacks of native rule are increased by remoteness from suitable markets.

Men who have served a cadetship on a good estate in Ceylon or Southern India, and who are unable to invest in these countries, would do well to consider the prospects offered them in the West Indies. With a capital of from £1,500 to £2,000, a good banana plantation might be established in British Honduras, which should bring in a return within some eighteen months of planting. Concurrently with bananas, coco-nuts, cacao, Liberian coffee and spices might be planted, and eventually a good property established of a permanent and remunerative character. With a large capital, say of £5,000 to £8,000 (and land at a dollar per acre), a sugar estate might be started; and the numerous other products gradually grouped around it for the more complete utilisation of the land, as well as for supplementing the resources of the planter.

For young men who have had no previous experience of a tropical country, it would be very undesirable for them to go out to British Honduras, unless they have made previous arrangements to place themselves for a year or two under the control of an experienced planter. Such men require to become acquainted with the ways of the country, and with the management of labour; as also to become inured to the climate and the somewhat rough and hard life of the pioneer in new lands. So that, apart from what knowledge they may have of the principles of agriculture, and of the cultivation of tropical plants, it is very important that new men should spend some time in the colony, and become thoroughly acquainted with it, before they invest their money.

If such men were to place themselves under experienced and successful planters, such as the managers of Regalia, Serpon, or Seven Hills Estates, and make arrangements to spend, say, twelve or eighteen months in learning the details of estate life, they would at the end of that time be in a position to invest their capital to the best advantage, and be prepared to undertake the management of their own property with every prospect of success.

I would be inclined to place £1,000 as the lowest sum a man should have to embark in fruit-growing in British Honduras. Many, already established in the colony, have started on much less, but they have had the advantage of local knowledge and experience to guide them. During the first year of a cadet's life, his expenses will probably be £120 to £150. He has to maintain himself for another year or two before any returns come in from his plantation: this will bring up his expenditure to some £350; and at the lowest calculation a plantation of fifty acres of bananas, with a small house for the manager, and some huts for the labourers, cannot cost less than £500 to £600. Hence it would appear that £1,000 is about the lowest sum required. It would be more advantageous to possess £2,000, as, in addition to bananas, coco-nuts might also be planted, which, as they require some five or six years to mature, should be put out during the first year of the planter's operations.

The great want of the colony would appear to be not merely

capital or labour, but a class of trustworthy and capable headmen or foremen to control and teach the ordinary Creole or Indian. The early history of the country has been unfavourable to the development of agricultural pursuits, and hence hardly a man in the colony is acquainted even with the most elementary principles of planting. The European manager or proprietor must therefore be prepared to teach and train his men, and give close and constant attention to every detail of estate work. Hence a man with a good practical knowledge of planting, acquired in other tropical countries, is the more likely to succeed in British Honduras; and next to him the young, able-bodied cadet, who is content to wait and to pick up his experience little by little under an older man, until he is qualified to embark on his own account.

The man without capital is evidently not required in British Honduras at present; in fact, there are no salaried appointments to which he could be appointed, and I would advise such to try the older and more settled colonies.

To men who have already been in the tropics it is needless to say much as regards the nature of the outfit most suitable for pioneering work in a new country. For cadets, the case is different. As a rule, young men arrive in the tropics with numberless things for which they can have no possible use. Either they bring out an elaborate outfit, composed entirely of fine, well-made clothes and thin boots, which the first day in the jungle will irretrievably spoil; or they come out booted, and spurred, and armed in such a fashion that they appear like amateur brigands. The chief requisites of a young planter are rather light, well-made boots, capable of keeping out wet, care being taken that they are not too heavy; a good pair of leather leggings, made to strap, not button; and a knicker-bocker suit—with or without a waistcoat—of tweed or cheviot. Two or three, or even four sets of these, with a good riding suit of whipcord, would be invaluable for everyday use, supplemented by a good waterproof coat, soft wideawake hat, and a solar helmet. As regards other clothes, each person should be guided by his own tastes and resources. For town wear, gentlemen in the tropics usually dress as in England in July and August: thin tweeds, light or dark in colour, are very serviceable, as also blue serges.

For river travelling or camping-out, a good waterproof rug, an ulster, or warm wrap, a mosquito net, a hammock, a useful gun, a machete or cutlass, a compass, and a few canteen utensils are most valuable. One of Davis's colonial saddles, with complete fittings, are essential where riding is not a luxury, but often the only means of travelling from place to place. For most other things, possibly the local stores are as advantageous as those in Europe; for if the risk of loss and damage is added to the expenses of agency, freight, insurance, and customs dues, the difference in price is not very great. Moreover, the colonial store possesses the advantage of supplying goods exactly suitable to the requirements of the country, and of placing them at the disposal of the planter in large or small quantities, as he may require them. For underclothing, fine flannel shirts, with loose easy collars, are the best for everyday wear, with a good supply of print and white shirts for evening or town wear. Drawers are looked upon by some as essential to keep out ticks and sand-flies; while a cholera-belt, or a strip of flannel worn round the loins, is decidedly useful when exposed to extremes of temperature and heavy rains, incidental to a planter's life. It is hardly necessary to state that although generally the weather along the coast is warm, there are periods of extreme cold felt in the interior, due to the cloudless skies and the rapid radiation of heat, when warm wraps are essential.

A very important element in the outfit of a tropical planter is a small medicine chest, containing a few of the most suitable remedies for cases of emergency likely to arise in the jungle. Speaking from my own experience of life in the tropics, there is nothing so generally useful and so likely to supply exactly what is required in the way of medicines as Kirby's "Miniature Dispensary," which is a small and very portable medicine chest costing only some 20s. Each chest is supplied with plain directions, or a guide to proper remedies for common ailments, accidents, and emergencies, and by means of this convenient addition to one's luggage I have been able to treat *immediately* the ailments of myself or my servants, which might have become, by delay, very serious. For the information of persons intending to go out to the tropics I may add that the "Miniature Dispensary" can be obtained from Messrs. H. & T. Kirby & Co., 14, Newman Street, Oxford Street, W.

The best time of year to arrive in British Honduras would be in the cool weather, after the October rains, and during what are generally termed there the winter months. Being entirely within the northern tropics the seasons follow in the order of those of England, with the exception that there are no well-defined differences, except in the matter of slight coolness, between summer and winter. A West Indian winter is still a time of bright sunny weather, a little tempered, however, by north winds, which render the early mornings and evenings quite cool. If the rains are not delayed, the months of November and December are the best to land in and begin life, as river travelling is easy and pleasant. For bush work it is better to choose the dry weather of February, March, and April, when riding through any portion of the colony is practically easy, and camping out unattended by many of the discomforts of the wet season.

APPENDIX.

List of Books and Serials suitable for Tropical Planters.

Books.

The **Treasury of Botany** : a Popular Dictionary of the Vegetable Kingdom. Longmans & Co., London.
Encyclopædia of the Industrial Arts, Manufactures, and Commercial Products. E. & F. N. Spon, London.
The Tropical Agriculturist. Porter, London.
Tropical Agriculture. Simmonds, London.
Notes on the Sugar-Cane and the Manufacture of Sugar in the West Indies. Anderson, Trinidad.
The Practical Sugar Planter. Wray, London.
New Commercial Plants, with directions how to grow them. Six numbers. Thomas Christy, F.L.S., London.
Chocolate and Cocoa : Growth and Culture, Manufacture, &c. Hewett, London.
Cacao : How to Grow and how to Cure it. Morris, London.
The Coffee Planter of St. Domingo. Laborie, London.
Coffee Planting in Southern India and Ceylon. Hull, London.
The Coffee Planter in Ceylon. Sabonadière, London.
Vanilla : its Cultivation in India. O'Conor, Calcutta.
Tropical Fibres : their Production and Economic Production. Squier, London.
Liberian Coffee : its History and Cultivation. Morris, Kingston, Jamaica.
The Cultivation of Liberian Coffee in the West Indies. Nicolls, London.
On the Cultivation of Coffee, Cardamom, Rubber-yielding Plants, &c., &c. (See Ceylon *Observer* Press Series of Handbooks). Haddon & Co., London.

SERIALS.

The Tropical Agriculturist. Monthly Magazine. Ferguson, Colombo, Ceylon; Haddon & Co., London.
Pharmaceutical Journal and Transactions. Monthly Record. London.
The Journal of the Society of Arts. Monthly Magazine. London.
The Technologist: a Monthly Record of Science, &c. London.
The Sugar-Cane: a Monthly Magazine. Manchester.
Agricultural Gazette of India. Calcutta.
The Planter's Gazette. Fortnightly. London.
The Gardener's Chronicle. Weekly. London.
The Colonies and India. Weekly. London.

For special information on British Honduras see:—

An Almanack of British Honduras for the year 1883: an annual publication compiled in the Colonial Secretary's Office, and printed at the Government Printing Office, Belize.
A Narrative of a Journey across the Unexplored Portion of British Honduras, with a short sketch of the History and Resources of the Colony. By Henry Fowler, Colonial Secretary. Belize, 1879.
On the History, Trade, and Natural Resources of British Honduras. A Paper read before the Society of Arts by Mr. Chief Justice Temple. *Journal of the Society of Arts*, January 11th, 1857.
Planting Enterprise in the West Indies. A Paper read before the Royal Colonial Institute, 12th June, 1883, by D. Morris, M.A., F.L.S., F.G.S. *Proceedings of the Royal Colonial Institute.* London: Sampson Low & Co., 1883.
British Honduras: An Historical and Descriptive Account of the Colony from its settlement, 1670. By Archibald Robertson Gibbs. London: Sampson Low & Co., 1883.

INDEX.

Acacia spadicifera, 84.
Acrocomia sclerocarpa, 68.
Acrostichum, 70.
Adiantum, 70.
Admiral Benbow, 2.
Advance system, 122.
Agave ixtli, 83.
Agriculture, 10.
Agricultural board, 129.
Akee, 113.
Allumanda, 14.
Alligators, 21.
Alligator-wood, 86.
All Pines, 8, 27.
Ancient ruins, 10.
Anona palustris, 86.
Ants, leaf-cutting, 24.
Area of colony, 5.
Armadillo, 21.
Arnatto, 85.
Arundo, 30.
Asplenium, 70.

BABOONS, 21.
Bactris horrida, 67.
Bahama grass, 14.
Baker's, 12.
Balise, 13.
Balsam of Tolu, 86.
Bambu, 11, 44.
Bananas, 16, 26, 92.
Barlee, Sir Fred. P., 17, 122.
Bay of Honduras, 3, 5.
Baymen, 3, 61.
Beaver Dam, 42.
Belize creole, 13, 15, 115.
—— harbour of, 15.
—— health of, 15.
—— river, 3, 5, 6, 9.
—— town of, 5, 6, 9, 10, 14, 41.
Big Falls, 11.
Birds, 21.

Bixa orellana, 85.
Blanconeaux, Mr., 50.
Blighia sapida, 113.
Boom, 12.
Botanic gardens, 131.
Boundaries, 1, 4, 5.
Brassovola, 69.
Bread-fruit, 111.
Bread-nut, 63.
Broken-ridge, 63.
Bromelia pita, 83.
Brosimum alicastrum, 63.
Brot, Mr. de, 35.
Building stone, 20.
Bulrush, 34, 87.
Burnaby's laws, 3.
Butcher Burn's Bank, 41.

CABBAGE PALM, 11, 34.
Cacao, 72, 93.
Calonictyon speciosum, 76.
Calophyllum calaba, 62.
Campeachy, 2.
Camphor, 106.
Candle-tree, 63.
Capoche, 88.
Carapa, 88.
Cardamoms, 107.
Caribs, 16, 32, 118.
Caribbean lily, 11.
—— sea, 5.
Cashaw, 63.
Cassava, 115.
Cassia diphylla, 67.
Castile Bank, 42.
Castilloa elastica, 74, 81.
Castor oil, 110.
Caves, 20.
Cay, Ambergris, Half-Moon, Hen and Chickens, Hicks, Hot, Northern Two, Saddle, St. George's, 6.
Cayo, 5, 6, 50.

Cays, 20, 53.
Cedar, 16, 61.
Cedrela odorata, 61.
Ceiba, 44.
Central America, 1, 9.
—— American rubber, 74, 81.
—— range, 9.
Chamædorea, 68, 69.
Chief Justice, 5.
Chinese, 16.
Chocho, 115.
Chrysobalanus, 32.
Chrysophyllum cainito, 111.
Church of England, 138.
Cinchona, 102.
Cinnamomum, 106.
City of Dallas, 39.
Clayton-Bulwer treaty, 2.
Climate, 9, 10, 133, 135.
Cloves, 110.
Coast, 6, 9.
Cockscomb mountains, 8, 9, 18.
Cockspur, 64, 84.
Coco-nut palm, 11.
—— cultivation of, 98.
Coco-nuts, 13, 14, 16, 27.
Coco-plum, 32.
Cocos, 115.
Coffee, Liberian, 96.
—— plantation at Cayo, 50.
Cohune-palm, 59, 60.
Cohune-ridge, 37, 58, 60.
Colonial secretary, 5, 10.
Colston Point, 27.
Columbus, 2.
Commerce Bight, 27.
Commissioners, 2, 4.
Conch, 22.
Conies, 21.
Constitution, 3, 4.
Cook, Captain, 3.
Coolies, 28, 120.
Copaifera officinalis, 86.
Coral islands, 5.
—— snake, 23.
Corkwood, 86.
Corosal, 6, 10.
Cost of living at Belize, 137.
Coyote, 20.
Cozumel, 2.

Crabboe, 56.
Crabs, 14.
Cramer's Bank, 41.
Creoles, 13, 32, 115.
Criminal court, 4.
Croton oil, 110.
Crown government, 4.
—— lands, 124.
Curassow, 21.
Curcuma longa, 109.
Cycnoches, 70.
Cynodon dactylon, 111.

DEEP RIVER, 34.
Deer, 21.
Desmoncus, 30, 68.
"Doctor," 52.
Don Zevallez, 3.

EAGLE, 22.
Egret, 22.
Elective assembly, 4.
England, 5, 9.
English cay, 6.
—— goods, 11.
Epidendrum, 69.
Eriobotrya japonica, 113.
Europeans, 9, 10, 13, 15.
Euterpe edulis, 68.
Executive council, 4, 5.
Expeditions, 18, 19.
Exports, 16.

FALLS, Big, 11; Garbutt's, 5.
False Bay, 31.
Ferns, 70.
Fibre plants, 83.
Fiddle-wood, 62.
Fig-trees, 11, 12.
Fish, 22.
Flamboyante, 14.
Flies, 23; bottlass, 23.
Flora, 53.
Fly on sugar-cane, 36.
Fodder plants, 110.
Food plants, 114.
Fowler, Mr., 9, 19.
Frontier, 5, 9, 10, 11, 13.
Fruit companies, 26, 124.
—— cultivation, 17, 113.

INDEX.

Fruits in general, 114.
Fustic, 16, 86.

Galeandra, 69.
Gale Creek, 42.
Gaol, 13.
Garbutt's Falls, 5.
Garcinia mangostana, 114.
Geological survey, 20, 132.
Geology, 54.
Gibonet, 21.
Gillett, Mr., 41, 45, 49.
Ginger, 108.
Glacial action, 55.
Gold, 18.
Government, 4, 5; lands, 4, 6, 125.
Governor, Lieutenant, 4, 5, 13.
Grasses, 110, 111.
Guaco, 86.
Guarana, 85.
Guatemala, 2, 5, 11, 19.
Guinea grass, 110.

Habenaria, 67.
Haha, 56.
Half-moon Cay, 6.
Harbour of Belize, 15.
Health of Belize, 15.
Hell-gates, 28.
Hevea brasiliensis, 80.
Highlands, 9.
Hints to settlers, 139.
Hippomane Mancinella, 87.
Historical sketch, 2, 3, 4.
Hondu river, 3, 6.
Honduras discovered, 2.
Horseradish-tree, 85.
Horses, 137.
Hot Cay, 6.
House-rent in Belize, 137.
Hunter, Mr. C. T., 27.
Hymenæa courbaril, 63.

IGUANA, 21.
Imports, 16.
Indian corn, 101.
Indians, 13.
—— Mosquito, 119.
—— Santa Cruz, 16.
—— Waikas, 119.

Indiarubber, export of, 16.
—— preparation of, 76.
Indiarubber-tree, 30, 74.
—— cultivation of, 81.
Indigofera anil, 85.
Institutions, 13.
Interior, 6.
Ipecacuanha, 108.
Island of Cozumel, 2.
Islands, Coral, 5.
Ixoras, 14.

JAGUAR, 20.
Jatropha curcas, 110.
John Young's pine-ridge, 41.
Jonathan Point, 31.

KARAMANI GUM, 85.

LABOUR SUPPLY, 28, 115.
—— laws, 120.
Lagoon, Crab Catch, 10.
—— New River, 10.
Lagoons, 5, 13.
Languages, 137.
Latitude, 9, 10.
Lawsonia inermis, 14.
Legislative council, 5.
Lemons, 98.
Lieutenant-Governor, 4, 5, 13.
Lighthouse, 6.
Limes, 6.
Limestone, 11, 20.
Livistona, 14.
Logwood, 16.
—— cutters, 2.
—— cutting, 3, 4, 48.
—— export of, 17.
—— trees, 61.
Loquat, 113.
Lunatic asylum, 13.

Maclura tinctoria, 86.
Mahogany, 16, 43, 61.
—— cutting, 4, 48.
—— export of, 17.
—— works, 10, 11, 47.
Mail communication, 126.
Maize, 101.
Manattee, 21; Bay, 25.

M

Manchineel-tree, 87.
Mango, 111.
Mangrove, 5, 33, 53.
Manihot Glaziovi, 80.
—— *utilissima*, 115.
Marble, 20.
Marriner, Captain, 25, 39, 40.
Meteorological observations, 136.
Mexican frontier, 5.
Mexico, 2.
Middle station, 11.
Mikania guaco, 86.
Military quarters, 14.
Minerals, 10, 18, 19.
Monkey Fall Savannah, 49.
Monkeys, 21.
Moon plant. 76.
Moringa, 85.
Morison, Mr. Wm., 35.
Mosquito coast, 1, 4.
Mosquito Indians, 119.
Mosquitoes, 23.
Mountain zone, 9.
Mountains, Cockscomb, 8, 9, 18.
Mount Hope, 21, 49.
—— Pleasant, 45.
Munroe doctrine, 2.
Myroxylon, 86.

NEGROES, 13.
Never Delay, 11.
New Orleans, 17, 126.
New River, 4.
North Stann Creek, 27.
Nutmegs, 104.

OAK, 56.
Ocelot, 20.
Oil plants, 109.
Old River, 10, 12.
Oleander, 14.
Oncidium, 69, 70.
Orange Walk (New River), 10.
—— (Old River), 11, 40, 45, 46, 52.
Oranges, 98.
Orchids, 34, 45, 69.
Oreodoxa oleracea, 33, 68.
—— *regia*, 14, 68.
Orgil, Mr., 39.
Osprey, 22.

Pachira aquatica, 85.
Palm, bay-leaf, 67.
—— bootan, 68.
—— cabbage, 12, 68.
—— climbing, 30, 68.
—— coco-nut, 11, 14, 98.
—— cohune, 59, 67.
—— give-and-take, 68.
—— gru-gru, or supa, 64, 68.
—— monkey-tail, 68.
—— no-give-massa, 68.
—— oil, 109.
—— pimento, 29, 34.
—— pocknoboy, 67.
—— royal, 14.
—— salt-water pimento, 69.
—— silver thatch, 68.
—— thatch, 14.
Palms, 67.
Pancratium, 11.
Panicum barbinode, 110.
—— *jumentorum*, 110.
Para grass, 110.
Paritium elatum, 62.
Parmentiera edulis, 63.
Parrots, 12.
Partridge, 22.
Paspalum distichum, 111.
Paullinia sorbilis, 85.
Peccary, 20.
Pepper, black, 107.
—— Jamaica, 105.
Persea gratissima, 113.
Peten, 11.
Physic-nut, 110.
Pimento, 105.
—— palm, 29, 34.
Pindar-nuts, 110.
Pine-apples, 102.
Pine-ridge, 26, 56.
—— distribution of, 57.
—— plants of, 57.
Pinus cubensis, 57, 58.
Pithecolobium ligustrum, 67.
—— *saman*, 111.
Pit-pan, 11, 29.
Placentia Point, 8, 31.
Plumeria alba, 14.
Point Ycacos, 33.
Ponta Gorda, 39.

INDEX.

Poor-house, 13.
Population, 15.
—— of Belize, 13.
Port Honduras, 34.
Potato, sweet, 115.
Precious stones, 20.
Prices of fruit, 17.
—— food, 137.
—— Crown lands, 125.
Prosopis juliflora, 63.
Provision-tree, 85.

QUAM, 22.
Quartz, gold-bearing, 19.
Quash, 21.
Quercus virens, 56.

RACOON, 21.
Railway proposals, 129.
Rapids, 11.
—— Gracias á Dios, 5.
Rattlesnakes, 22.
Rats, 14.
Regalia sugar estate, 27.
Religious denominations, 137.
Revenue, 16.
Rice, 100.
Ricinus communis, 110.
Rio Grande, 37.
River Belize, or Old, 5, 6, 9, 10, 12, 40, 46.
—— Deep, 19, 34.
—— Hondu, 3, 10, 57.
—— Manattee, 9.
—— Monkey, 31, 32.
—— Mullin's, 9, 25.
—— New, 4, 10, 57.
—— Sarstoon, 5, 39.
—— Sibun, 9, 25, 41, 42, 46.
—— Sittee, 18, 27, 29.
—— Stann Creek, 31.
—— system, 10, 54.
Roaring Creek, 49.
Rock Dondo, 11.
Rocky Point, 6.
Rosewood, 16.
Ross, Mr. Reginald, 27.
Royal marriage, 12.
Rubber-tree, 30, 74, 81.
Rum, 16.

TABASCO CACAO, 73.
Tapir, 21.
Tarantula, 23.
Tea, 103.
Tea-kettle, 49, 52.
Telegraphic communication, 128.
Temperature, 9, 136.
Theobroma angustifolia, 72.
—— *cacao*, 72.
Thrinax, 14.
—— *argentea*, 68.
Tie-ties, 45.
Tiger run, 49.
Timber, 16, 62.
Timber-trees: axemaster, bazilletto, bull-hoof, cabbage bark, 62 ; cashaw, 63 ; cedar, 16, 29 ; dogwood, fiddle-wood, 62 ; fustic, 16 ; grape, half-crown, ironwood, lignum vitæ (bastard), 62 ; locust, 63 ; mahoe, 62 ; mahogany, 16, 29, 61 ; palmalata, pigeon-wood, polewood, 62 ; rose-wood, 16, 29, 62 ; salmwood, 62 ; Santa Maria, 18, 50, 62 ; sappodilla, 62 ; logwood, 16, 61 ; wynaka, 62 ; yemeri, 31 ; ziricote, 62.
Tobacco, 102.
Tococa coriacea, 84.
Toledo settlement, 37, 136.
Tomatoes, 116.
Tortoise, 22.
Trade, 16.
—— winds, 9.
Travers, Mr., 51.
Treaty of Madrid, 2.
—— Paris, 3.
—— Versailles, 3.
Trinidad cacao, 72.
Trophis americana, 63.
Turkeys, 21.
Turmeric, 108.
Turtle, 16, 22.
Two-headed cabbage, 11.

UNEXPLORED TERRITORY, 9.
United Kingdom, 16.
—— States, 2, 9, 16.

VALLEY OF OLD RIVER, 11.
Vanilla, 50, 81.

INDEX.

Vanilla planifolia, 81.
Vivenot, M., 50.
Volcanic rocks, 19.
Vulture, 22.

WAGES, 28, 120.
Warree, 20.
West India Islands, 5.
Wild animals, 5.
Williamson, Hon. A., 33, 40, 46.

Wood-cutting, 17.

YAMS, 114.
Ycacos Point, 33.
Yucatan, 1, 5, 6.

Zamia, 34, 87.
Zea mays, 101.
Zingiber officinarum, 10.
Ziricote, 62.

www.ingramcontent.com/pod-product-compliance
Lightning Source LLC
Chambersburg PA
CBHW030259170426
43202CB00009B/806